REDESIGNING AI

WORK, DEMOCRACY, AND JUSTICE IN THE AGE OF AUTOMATION

in collaboration with
THE PARTNERSHIP ON AI

made possible by a generous grant from
THE WILLIAM AND FLORA HEWLETT FOUNDATION

Redesigning AI *is* Boston Review *Forum 18 (46.2)*

Redesigning AI *is published in cooperation with the AI and Shared Prosperity Initiative of the Partnership on AI, a nonprofit working across industry, academia, and civil society to explore the social implications of AI and foster broad, equitable benefit from its applications. For more info visit:* partnershiponai.org/shared-prosperity

Nichola Lowe's essay is adapted from Putting Skill to Work: How to Create Good Jobs in Uncertain Times. *Copyright 2021 by The MIT Press. Used with permission.*

To become a member, visit
bostonreview.net/membership/

For questions about donations and major gifts,
contact Dan Manchon, dan@bostonreview.net

For questions about memberships, call 877-406-2443
or email Customer_Service@bostonreview.info.

Boston Review
PO Box 390568
Cambridge, MA 02139

ISSN: 0734-2306 / ISBN: 978-1-946511-62-1

CONTENTS

ESSAYS

EDITORS' NOTE

Joshua Cohen & Deborah Chasman

OUR WORLD is increasingly powered by artificial intelligence. The singularity is not here, but sophisticated machine-learning algorithms are—revolutionizing medicine and transport; transforming jobs and markets; reshaping where we eat, who we meet, what we read, and how we learn. At the same time, the promises of AI are increasingly overshadowed by its perils, from unemployment and disinformation to powerful new forms of bias and surveillance.

Leading off a forum that explores these issues, economist Daron Acemoglu argues that the threats—especially for work and democracy—are indeed serious, but the future is not settled. Just as technological development promoted broadly shared gains in the three decades following World War II, so AI can create inclusive prosperity and bolster democratic freedoms. Setting it to that task won't be easy, but it can be achieved through thoughtful government policy, the redirection of professional and industry norms, and robust democratic oversight.

Respondents to Acemoglu—economists, computer scientists, labor activists, and others—broaden the conversation by debating the role new technology plays in economic inequality, the range of algorithmic harms facing workers and citizens, and the additional steps that can be taken to ensure a just future for AI. Some ask how we can transform the way we design AI to create better jobs for workers. Others urge that we need new participatory methods in research, development, and deployment to address the unfair burdens AI bias has already imposed on vulnerable and marginal populations. Others argue that changes in social norms won't happen until workers have a seat at the table.

Contributions beyond the forum expand the aperture, exploring the impact of new technology on medicine and care work, the importance of workplace training in the AI economy, and the ethical case for not building certain forms of AI in the first place. In "Stop Building Bad AI," Annette Zimmermann challenges the belief that something designed badly can later be repaired and improved, an industry-wide version of the Facebook motto to "move fast and break things." She questions whether companies will police themselves, and instead calls for new frameworks for determining what kinds of AI are too risky to be designed in the first place.

What emerges from this remarkable mix of perspectives is a deeper understanding of the current challenges of AI and a rich, constructive, morally urgent vision for redirecting its course.

FORUM

REDESIGNING
AI

Daron Acemoglu

ARTIFICIAL INTELLIGENCE (AI) is not likely to make humans redundant. Nor will it create superintelligence anytime soon. But, like it or not, AI technologies and intelligent systems will make huge advances in the next two decades—revolutionizing medicine, entertainment, and transport; transforming jobs and markets; enabling many new products and tools; and vastly increasing the amount of information that governments and companies have about individuals. Should we cherish and look forward to these developments, or fear them?

There are reasons to be concerned. Current AI research is too narrowly focused on making advances in a limited set of domains and pays insufficient attention to its disruptive effects on the very fabric of society. If AI technology continues to develop along its current path, it is likely to create social upheaval for at least two reasons. For one, AI will affect the future of jobs. Our current trajectory automates work to an excessive degree while refusing to invest in human productivity; further advances will displace workers and fail to create new opportunities (and, in the process, miss out on AI's full potential to enhance productivity). For another, AI may undermine democracy and individual freedoms.

Each of these directions is alarming, and the two together are ominous. Shared prosperity and democratic political participation do not just critically reinforce each other: they are the two backbones of our modern society. Worse still, the weakening of democracy makes formulating solutions to the adverse labor market and distributional effects of AI much more difficult. These dangers have only multiplied during the COVID-19 crisis. Lockdowns, social distancing, and workers' vulnerability to the virus have given an additional boost to the drive for automation, with the majority of U.S. businesses reporting plans for more automation.

None of this is inevitable, however. The direction of AI development is not preordained. It can be altered to increase human productivity, create jobs and shared prosperity, and protect and bolster democratic freedoms—if we modify our approach. In order to redirect AI research toward a more productive path, we need to look at AI funding and regulation, the norms and priorities of AI researchers, and the societal oversight guiding these technologies and their applications.

Our Modern Compact

THE POSTWAR ERA witnessed a bewildering array of social and economic changes. Many social scientists in the first half of the twentieth century predicted that modern economies would lead to rising inequality and discontent, ultimately degenerating into various types of authoritarian governments or endless chaos.

The events of the interwar years seemed to confirm these gloomy forecasts. But in postwar Western Europe and North America—and several other parts of the globe that adopted similar economic and political institutions—the tide turned. After 1945 industrialized nations came to experience some of their best decades in terms of economic growth and social cohesion—what the French called *Les Trente Glorieuses*, the thirty glorious years. And that growth was not only rapid but also broadly shared. Over the first three decades after World War II, wages grew rapidly for all workers in the United States, regardless of education, gender, age, or race. Though this era was not without its political problems (it coincided with civil rights struggles in the United States), democratic politics worked: there was quite a bit of bipartisanship when it came to legislation, and Americans felt that they had a voice in politics. These two aspects of the postwar era were critical for social peace—a large fraction of the population understood that they were benefiting from the economic system and felt they had a voice in how they were governed.

How did this relative harmony come about? Much of the credit goes to the trajectory of technological progress. The great economist John Maynard Keynes, who recognized the fragility of social peace in the face of economic hardship more astutely than most others, famously predicted in 1929 that economic growth would create increasing joblessness in the twentieth century. Keynes understood that there were tremendous opportunities for industrial automation—replacing human workers with machines—and concluded that declining demand for human labor was an ineluctable consequence of technological progress. As he put it: "We are being afflicted with a new disease of which . . . [readers] . . . will hear a great deal in the years to come—namely, technological unemployment."

Yet the technologies of the next half century turned out to be rather different from what Keynes had forecast. Demand for human labor grew and then grew some more. Keynes wasn't wrong about the forces of automation; mechanization of agriculture—substituting harvesters and tractors for human labor—caused massive dislocation and displacement for almost half of the workforce in the United States. Crucially, however, mechanization was accompanied by the introduction of new tasks, functions, and activities for humans. Agricultural mechanization was followed by rapid industrial automation, but this too was counterbalanced by other technological advances that created new tasks for workers. Today the majority of the workforce in all industrialized nations engages in tasks that did not exist when Keynes was writing (think of all the tasks involved in modern education, health care, communication, entertainment, back-office work, design, technical work on factory floors, and almost all of the service sector). Had it not been for these new tasks, Keynes would have been right. They not only spawned plentiful jobs but also generated demand for a diverse set of skills, underpinning the shared nature of modern economic growth.

Acemoglu

Labor market institutions—such as minimum wages, collective bargaining, and regulations introducing worker protection—greatly contributed to shared prosperity. But without the more human-friendly aspects of technological change, they would not have generated broad-based wage growth. If there were rapid advances in automation technology and no other technologies generating employment opportunities for most workers, minimum wages and collective wage demands would have been met with yet more automation. However, when these institutional arrangements protecting and empowering workers coexist with technological changes increasing worker productivity, they encourage the creation of "good jobs"—secure jobs with high wages. It makes sense to build long-term relationships with workers and pay them high wages when they are rapidly becoming more productive. It also makes sense to create good jobs and invest in worker productivity when labor market institutions rule out the low-wage path. Hence, technologies boosting human productivity and labor market institutions protecting workers were mutually self-reinforcing.

Indeed, good jobs became a mainstay of many postwar economies, and one of the key reasons that millions of people felt they were getting their fair share from the growth process—even if their bosses and some businessmen were becoming fabulously rich in the process.

Why was technology fueling wage growth? Why didn't it just automate jobs? Why was there a slew of new tasks and activities for workers, bolstering wage and employment growth? We don't know for sure. Existing evidence suggests a number of factors that may have helped boost the demand for human labor. In the decades following World War II, U.S. businesses operated in a broadly competitive environment. The biggest conglomerates of the early twentieth century had been broken up by Progressive Era reforms, and those that became dominant in the second half of the century, such as AT&T, faced similar antitrust action. This competitive environment produced a ferocious appetite for new technologies, including those that raised worker productivity.

These productivity enhancements created just the type of advantage firms were pining for in order to surge ahead of their rivals. Technology was not a gift from the heavens, of course. Businesses invested heavily in technology and they benefited from government support. It wasn't just the eager investments in higher education during the Sputnik era (lest the United States fall behind the Soviet Union). It was also the government's role as a funding source, major purchaser of new technologies, and director and coordinator for research efforts. Via funding from the National Science Foundation, the National Institutes of Health, research and development tax credits, and perhaps even more importantly the Department of Defense, the government imprinted its long-term perspective on many of the iconic technologies of the era, including the Internet, computers, nanotechnology, biotech, antibiotics, sensors, and aviation technologies.

The United States also became more democratic during this period. Reforms during the Progressive and New Deal Eras reduced the direct control of large corporations and wealthy tycoons over the political process. The direct election of senators, enacted in 1913 in the Seventeenth Amendment, was an important step in this process. Then came the cleaning up of machine politics in many northern cities, a process that took several decades in the first half of the century. Equally important was the civil rights movement, which ended some of the most undemocratic aspects of U.S. politics (even if this is still a work in progress). Of course there were many fault lines, and not just Black Americans but many groups did not have sufficient voice in politics. All the same when political scientist Robert Dahl set out to investigate "who governs" local politics in New Haven, the answer wasn't an established party or a well-defined elite. Power was pluralistic, and the involvement of regular people in politics was key for the governance of the city.

Democracy and shared prosperity thus bolstered each other during this epoch. Democratic politics strengthened labor market institutions protecting workers and efforts to increase worker productivity, while shared prosperity simultaneously increased the legitimacy of the democratic system. And this trend was robust: despite myriad cultural and institutional differences, Western Europe, Canada, and Japan followed remarkably similar trajectories to that of the United States, based on rapid productivity growth, shared prosperity, and democratic politics.

The World Automation is Making

WE LIVE in a very different world today. Wage growth since the late 1970s has been much slower than during the previous three decades. And this growth has been anything but shared. While wages for workers at the very top of the income distribution—those in the highest tenth percentile of earnings or those with postgraduate degrees—have continued to grow, workers with a high school diploma or less have seen their real earnings fall. Even college graduates have gone through lengthy periods of little real wage growth.

Many factors have played a role in this turnaround. The erosion of the real value of the minimum wage, which has fallen by more than 30 percent since 1968, has been instrumental in the wage declines at the bottom of the distribution. With the disappearance of trade unions from much of the private sector, wages also lagged behind productivity growth. Simultaneously, the enormous increase in trade with China led to the closure of many businesses and large job losses in low-tech manufacturing industries such as textiles, apparel, furniture, and toys. Equally defining has been the new direction of technological progress. While in the four decades after World War II automation and new tasks contributing to labor demand went hand-in-hand, a very different technological tableau began in the 1980s—a lot more automation and a lot less of everything else.

Automation acted as the handmaiden of inequality. New technologies primarily automated the more routine tasks in clerical occupations and on factory floors. This meant the demand and wages of workers specializing in blue-collar jobs and some clerical functions declined. Meanwhile professionals in managerial, engineering, finance, consulting, and design occupations flourished—both because they were essential to the success of new technologies and because they benefited from the automation of tasks that complemented their own work. As automation gathered pace, wage gaps between the top and the bottom of the income distribution magnified.

Acemoglu

The causes of this broad pattern—more automation and less effort directed toward increasing worker productivity—are not well understood. To be sure much of this predates AI. The rapid automation of routine jobs started with applications of computers, databases, and electronic communication in clerical jobs and with numerical control in manufacturing, and it accelerated with the spread of industrial robots. With breakthroughs in digital technologies, automation may have become technologically easier. However, equally (if not more) important are changes in policy and the institutional and policy environments. Government funding for research—especially the type of blue-sky research leading to the creation of new tasks—dried up. Labor market institutions that pushed for good jobs weakened. A handful of companies with business models focused on automation came to dominate the economy. And government tax policy started favoring capital and automation. Whatever the exact mechanisms, technology became less favorable to labor and more focused on automation.

AI is the next act in this play. The first serious research into AI started in the 1950s, with ambitious and, as it turned out, unrealistic goals. The AI pioneers keenly understood the power of computation and thought that creating intelligent machines was a challenging but achievable aspiration. Two of the early luminaries, Herbert Simon and Allen Newell, said in 1957: "There are now in the world machines that think, that learn and that create. Moreover, their ability to do these things is going to increase rapidly until—in a visible future—the range of problems they can handle will be coextensive with the range to which the human mind has been applied." But these hopes were soon dashed. It was one thing to program binary operations for fast computation—a task at which machines had well exceeded human capacities by the early 1950s. It was something completely different to have machines perform more complex tasks, including image recognition, classification, language processing, reasoning, and problem-solving. The euphoria and funding for the field dwindled, and AI winter(s) followed.

In the 1990s AI won renewed enthusiasm, albeit with altered ambitions. Rather than having machines think and understand exactly like humans, the new aim was to use cheaply available computation power and the vast amounts of data collected by sensors, present in books and online, and voluntarily given by individuals. The breakthrough came when we figured out how to turn many of the services we wanted into prediction problems. Modern statistical methods, including various types of machine learning, could be applied to the newly available, large, unstructured datasets to perform prediction-based tasks cheaply and effectively. This meant that the path of least resistance for the economic applications of AI was (algorithmic) automation—adapting pattern recognition, object classification, and statistical prediction into applications that could take over many of the repetitive and simple cognitive tasks millions of workers were performing.

What started as an early trend became the norm. Many experts now forecast that the majority of occupations will be fundamentally affected by AI in the decades to come. AI will also replace more skilled tasks, especially in accounting, finance, medical diagnosis, and mid-level management. Nevertheless current AI applications are still primarily replacing relatively simple tasks performed by low-wage workers.

The State of Democracy and Liberty

ALONGSIDE THIS STORY of economic woes, democracy hasn't fared too well, either—across both the developed and the developing world. Three factors have been especially important for U.S. democracy over the last thirty years.

First, polarization has increased considerably. In the decades that followed World War II, U.S. lawmakers frequently crossed the aisle and supported bills from the other party. This rarely occurs today. Polarization makes effective policy-making much harder—legislation to deal with urgent challenges becomes harder to pass and, when it does pass, it lacks the necessary legitimacy. This was painfully obvious, for example, in the efforts to enact a comprehensive health care reform to control rising costs and provide coverage to millions of Americans who did not have access to health insurance.

Second, the traditional media model, with trusted and mostly balanced sources, came undone. Cable news networks and online news sources have rendered the electorate more polarized and less willing to listen to counterarguments, making democratic discourse and bipartisan policy-making even more difficult.

Third, the role of money in politics has increased by leaps and bounds. As political scientists Larry Bartels and Martin Gilens have documented, even before the fateful Supreme Court decision on

Citizens United in 2010 opened the floodgates to corporate money, the richest Americans and the largest corporations had become disproportionately influential in shaping policy via lobbying efforts, campaign contributions, their outsize social status, and their close connections with politicians.

AI only magnified these fault lines. Though we are still very much in the early stages of the digital remaking of our politics and society, we can already see some of the consequences. AI-powered social media, including Facebook and Twitter, have already completely transformed political communication and debate. AI has enabled these platforms to target users with individualized messages and advertising. Even more ominously, social media has facilitated the spread of disinformation—contributing to polarization, lack of trust in institutions, and political rancor. The Cambridge Analytica scandal illustrates the dangers. The company acquired the private information of about 50 million individuals from data shared by around 270,000 Facebook users. It then used these data to design personalized and targeted political advertising in the Brexit referendum and the 2016 U.S. presidential election. Many more companies are now engaged in similar activities, with more sophisticated AI tools. Moreover, recent research suggests that standard algorithms used by social media sites such as Facebook reduce users' exposure to posts from different points of view, further contributing to the polarization of the U.S. public.

Other emerging applications of AI may be even more threatening to democracy and liberty around the world. Basic pattern recognition techniques are already powerful enough to enable governments and companies to monitor individual behavior, political views, and communication. For example, the Chinese Communist Party has long relied on these technologies for identifying and stamping out online dissent and opposition, for mass surveillance, and for controlling political activity in parts of the country where there is widespread opposition to its rule (such as Xinjiang and Tibet). As Edward Snowden's revelations laid bare, the U.S. government eagerly used similar techniques to collect massive amounts of data from the communications of both foreigners and American citizens. Spyware programs—such as Pegasus, developed by the Israeli firm NSO Group, and the Da Vinci and Galileo platforms of the Italian company Hacking Team—enable users to take control of the data of individuals thousands of miles away, break encryption, and remotely track private communications. Future AI capabilities will go far beyond these activities.

Another area of considerable concern is facial recognition, currently one of the most active fields of research within AI. Though facial recognition technology has legitimate uses in personal security and defense against terrorism, its commercial applications remain unproven. Much of the demand for this technology originates from mass surveillance programs.

With AI-powered technologies already able to collect information about individual behavior, track communications, and recognize faces and voices, it is not far-fetched to imagine that many governments will be better positioned to control dissent and discourage opposition. But the effects of these technologies may well go beyond silencing governments' most vocal critics. With the knowledge that such technologies are monitoring their every behavior, individuals will be discouraged from voicing criticism and may gradually reduce their participation in civic organizations and political activity. And with the increasing use of AI in military technologies, governments may be further empowered to act (even more) despotically toward their own citizens—as well as more aggressively toward external foes.

Individual dissent is the mainstay of democracy and social liberty, so these potential developments and uses of AI technology should alarm us all.

The AI Road Not Taken

MUCH OF THE DIAGNOSIS I have presented thus far is not new. Many decry the disruption that automation has already produced and is likely to cause in the future. Many are also concerned about the deleterious effects new technologies might have on individual liberty and democratic procedure. But the majority of these commentators view such concerns with a sense of inevitability—they believe that it is in the very nature of AI to accelerate automation and to enable governments and companies to control individuals' behavior.

Yet society's march toward joblessness and surveillance is not inevitable. The future of AI is still open and can take us in many different directions. If we end up with powerful tools of surveillance and ubiquitous automation (with not enough tasks left for humans to perform), it will be because we *chose* that path.

Acemoglu

Where else could we go? Even though the majority of AI research has been targeted toward automation in the production domain, there are plenty of new pastures where AI could complement humans. It can increase human productivity most powerfully by creating new tasks and activities for workers.

Let me give a few examples. The first is education, an area where AI has penetrated surprisingly little thus far. Current developments, such as they are, go in the direction of automating teachers—for example, by implementing automated grading or online resources to replace core teaching tasks. But AI could also revolutionize education by empowering teachers to adapt their material to the needs and attitudes of diverse students in real time. We already know that what works for one individual in the classroom may not work for another; different students find different elements of learning challenging. AI in the classroom can make teaching more adaptive and student-centered, generate distinct new teaching tasks, and, in the process, increase the productivity of—and the demand for—teachers.

The situation is very similar in health care, although this field has already witnessed significant AI investment. Up to this point, however, there have been few attempts to use AI to provide new, real-time, adaptive services to patients by nurses, technicians, and doctors. Similarly, AI in the entertainment sector can go a long way toward creating new, productive tasks for workers. Intelligent systems can greatly facilitate human learning and training in most occupations and fields by making adaptive technical and contextual information available on demand. Finally, AI can be combined with augmented and virtual reality to provide new productive opportunities to workers in blue-collar and technical occupations. For example, it can enable them to achieve a higher degree of precision so that they can collaborate with robotics technology and perform integrated design tasks.

In all of these areas, AI can be a powerful tool for deploying the creativity, judgment, and flexibility of humans rather than simply automating their jobs. It can help us protect their privacy and freedom, too. Plenty of academic research shows how emerging technologies—differential privacy, adversarial neural cryptography, secure multiparty computation, and homomorphic encryption, to name a few—can protect privacy and detect security threats and snooping, but this research is still marginal to commercial products and services. There is also growing awareness among both the public and the AI community that new technologies can harm public discourse, freedom, and democracy. In this climate many are demanding a concerted effort to use AI for good. Nevertheless it is remarkable how much of AI research still focuses on applications that automate jobs and increase the ability of governments and companies to monitor and manipulate individuals. This can and needs to change.

The Market Illusion

ONE OBJECTION to the argument I have developed is that it is unwise to mess with the market. Who are we to interfere with the innovations and technological breakthroughs the market is generating? Wouldn't intervening sacrifice productivity growth and even risk our technological vibrancy? Aren't we better off just letting the market mechanism deliver the best technologies and then use other tools, such as tax-based redistribution or universal basic income, to make sure that everybody benefits?

The answer is no, for several reasons. First, it isn't clear that the market is doing a great job of selecting the right technologies. It is true that we are in the midst of a period of prodigious technological creativity, with new breakthroughs and applications invented every day. Yet Robert Solow's thirty-year-old quip about computers—that they are "everywhere but in the productivity statistics"—is even more true today. Despite these mind-boggling inventions, current productivity growth is strikingly slow compared to the decades that followed World War II. This sluggishness is clear from the standard statistic that economists use for measuring how much the technological capability of the economy is expanding—the growth of total factor productivity (TFP). TFP growth answers a simple question: If we kept the amount of labor and capital resources we are using constant from one year to the next, and only our technological capabilities changed, how much would aggregate income grow? TFP growth in much of the industrialized world was rapid during the decades that followed World War II, and has fallen sharply since then. In the United States, for example, the average TFP growth was close to 2 percent a year between 1920 and 1970, and has averaged only a little above 0.5 percent a year over the last three decades. So the case that the market is doing a fantastic job of expanding our productive capacity isn't ironclad.

The argument that we should rely on the market for setting the direction of technological change is weak as well. In the terminology of economics, innovation creates significant positive "externalities": when a company or a researcher innovates, much of the benefits accrue to others. This is doubly so for technologies that create new tasks. The beneficiaries are often workers whose wages increase (and new firms that later find the right organizational structures and come up with creative products to make use of these new tasks). But these benefits are not part of the calculus of innovating firms and researchers. Ordinary market forces—which fail to take account of externalities—may therefore deter the types of technologies that have the greatest social value.

This same reasoning is even more compelling when new products produce *noneconomic* costs and benefits. Consider surveillance technologies. The demand for surveillance from repressive (and even some democratic-looking) governments may be great, generating plenty of financial incentives for firms and researchers to invest in facial recognition and snooping technologies. But the erosion of liberties is a notable noneconomic cost that it is often not taken into account. A similar point holds for automation technologies: it is easy to ignore the vital role that good, secure, and high-paying jobs play in making people feel fulfilled. With all of these externalities, how can we assume that the market will get things right?

Market troubles multiply further still when there are competing technological paradigms, as in the field of AI. When one paradigm is ahead of the others, both researchers and companies are tempted to herd on that leading paradigm, even if another one is more productive. Consequently, when the wrong paradigm surges ahead, it becomes very difficult to switch to more promising alternatives.

Last but certainly not least, innovation responds not just to economic incentives but also to norms. What researchers find acceptable, exciting, and promising is not purely a function of economic reward. Social norms play a key role by shaping researchers' aims as well as their moral compasses. And if the norms within the research area do not reflect our social objectives, the resulting technological change will not serve society's best interests.

All of these reasons cast doubt on the wisdom of leaving the market to itself. What's more, the measures that might be thought to compensate for a market left to itself—redistribution via taxes and the social safety net—are both insufficient and unlikely to work. We certainly need a better safety net. (The COVID-19 pandemic has made that even clearer.) But if we do not generate meaningful employment opportunities—and thus a viable social purpose—for most people in society, how can democracy work? And if democracy doesn't work, how can we enact such redistributive measures—and how can we be sure that they will remain in place in the future?

Even worse, building shared prosperity based predominantly on redistribution is a fantasy. There is no doubt that redistribution—via a progressive tax system and a robust social safety net—has been an important pillar of shared prosperity in much of the twentieth century (and high-quality public education has been critical). But it has been a supporting pillar, not the main engine of shared prosperity. Jobs, and especially good jobs, have been much more central, bolstered by productivity growth and labor market institutions supporting high wages. We can see this most clearly from the experiences of Nordic countries, where productivity growth, job creation, and shared gains in the labor market have been the bulwark of their social democratic compact. Industry-level wage agreements between trade unions and business associations set an essentially fixed wage for the same job throughout an industry. These collective agreements produced high and broadly equal wages for workers in similar roles. More importantly the system encouraged productivity growth and the creation of a plentiful supply of good jobs because, with wages largely fixed at the industry level, firms got to keep higher productivity as profits and had strong incentives to innovate and invest.

Who Controls AI?

IF WE ARE GOING to redirect intelligent systems research, we first have to understand what determines the current direction of research. Who controls AI?

Of course nobody single-handedly controls research, and nobody sets the direction of technological change. Nonetheless, compared to many other technological platforms—where we see support and leadership from different government agencies, academic researchers with diverse backgrounds and visions, and scores of research labs pushing in distinct directions—AI influence is concentrated in the hands of a few key players. A handful of tech giants, all focused on algorithmic automation—Google (Alphabet), Facebook, Amazon, Microsoft, Netflix, Ali Baba, and Baidu—account for the majority of money spent on AI research. (According to a recent McKinsey report, they are responsible for about $20 to $30 billion of the $26 to $39 billion in total private AI investment expenditures worldwide.) Government funding pales in comparison.

While hundreds of universities have vibrant, active departments and labs working on AI, machine learning, and big data, funding from major corporations shapes the direction of academic research, too. As government support for academic research has declined, corporations have come to play a more defining role in academic funding. Even more consequential might be the fact that there is now a revolving door between corporations and universities, with major researchers consulting for the private sector and periodically leaving their academic posts to take up positions in technology companies working on AI.

But the situation may actually be even worse, as leading technology companies are setting the agenda of research in three other significant ways. First, via both their academic relations and their philanthropic arms, tech companies are directly influencing the curriculum and AI fields at leading universities. Second, these companies and their charismatic founders and CEOs have loud voices in Washington, D.C., and in the priorities of funding agencies—the agencies that shape academic passions. Third, students wishing to specialize in AI-related fields often aspire to work for one of the major tech companies or for startups that are usually working on technologies that they can sell to these companies. Universities must respond to the priorities of their students, which means they are impelled to nourish connections with major tech companies.

This isn't to say that thinking in the field of AI is completely uniform. In an area that attracts hundreds of thousands of bright minds, there will always be a diversity of opinions and approaches—and some who are deeply aware that AI research has social consequences and bears a social responsibility. Nevertheless it is striking how infrequently AI researchers question the emphasis on automation. Too few researchers are using AI to create new jobs for humans or protect individuals from the surveillance of governments and companies.

How to Redirect AI

THESE ARE TROUBLING TRENDS. But even if I have convinced you that we need to redirect AI, how exactly can we do it?

The answer, I believe, lies in developing a three-pronged approach. Government policy, funding, and leadership are critical. These three prongs are well illustrated by past successes in redirecting technological change toward socially beneficial areas. For instance, in the context of energy generation and use, there have been tremendous advances in low- or zero-carbon emission technologies, even if we are still far from stemming climate change. These advances owe much to three simultaneous and connected developments. First, government policies produced a measurement framework to understand the amount of carbon emitted by different types of activities and determine which technologies were clean. Based on this framework, government policy (at least in some countries) started taxing and limiting carbon emissions. Then, even more consequentially, governments used research funding and intellectual leadership to redirect technological change toward clean sources of energy—such as solar, wind, and geothermal—and innovations directly controlling greenhouse gas emissions. Second, all this coincided with a change in norms. Households became willing to pay more to reduce their own carbon footprint—for example, by purchasing electric vehicles or using clean sources of energy themselves. They also started putting social pressure on others to do the same. Even more consequential were households' demands that their employers limit pollution. Third, all of this was underpinned by democratic oversight and pressure. Governments acted because voters insisted that they act; companies changed (even if, in some instances, these changes were illusory) because their employees and customers demanded change and because society at large turned the spotlight on them.

The same three-pronged approach can work in AI: government involvement, norms shifting, and democratic oversight.

First, government policy, funding, and leadership are critical. To begin with, we must remove policy distortions that encourage excessive automation and generate an inflated demand for surveillance technologies. Governments are the most important buyers of AI-based surveillance technologies. Even if it will be difficult to convince many security services to give up on these technologies, democratic oversight can force them to do so. As I already noted, government policy is also fueling the adoption and development of new automation technologies. For example, the U.S. tax code imposes tax rates around 25 percent on labor but less than 5 percent on equipment and software, effectively subsidizing corporations to install machinery and use software to automate work. Removing these distortionary incentives would go some way toward refocusing technological change away from automation. But it won't be enough. We need a more active government role to support and coordinate research efforts toward the types of technologies that are most socially beneficial and that are most likely to be undersupplied by the market.

As with climate change, such an effort necessitates a clear focus on measuring and determining which types of AI applications are most beneficial. For surveillance and security technologies, it is feasible, if not completely straightforward, to define which technological applications will strengthen the ability of companies and authoritarian governments to snoop on people and manipulate their behavior. It may be harder in the area of automation—how do you distinguish an AI automation application from one that leads to new tasks and activities for humans? For government policy to redirect research, these guidelines need to be in place before the research is undertaken and technologies are adopted. This calls for a better measurement framework—a tall order, but not a hopeless task. Existing theoretical and empirical work on the effects of automation and new tasks shows that they have very distinct effects on the labor share of value added (meaning how much of the value added created by a firm or industry goes to labor). Greater automation reduces the labor share, while new tasks increase it. Measuring the sum of the work-related consequences of new AI technologies via their impact on the labor share is, therefore, one promising avenue. Based on this measurement framework, policy can support technologies that tend to increase the labor share rather than those boosting profits at the expense of labor.

Acemoglu

Second, we must pay attention to norms. In the same way that millions of employees demand that their companies reduce their carbon footprint—or that many nuclear physicists would not be willing to work on developing nuclear weapons—AI researchers should become more aware of, more sensitive to, and more vocal about the social consequences of their actions. But the onus is not just on them. We all need to identify and agree on what types of AI applications contribute to our social ills. A clear consensus on these questions may then trigger self-reinforcing changes in norms as AI researchers and firms feel the social pressure from their families, friends, and society at large.

Third, all of this needs to be embedded in democratic governance. It is easier for the wrong path to persist when decisions are made without transparency and by a small group of companies, leaders, and researchers not held accountable to society. Democratic input and discourse are vital for breaking that cycle.

We are nowhere near a consensus on this, and changes in norms and democratic oversight remain a long way away. Nonetheless such a transformation is not impossible. We may already be seeing the beginning of a social awakening. For example, NSO Group's Pegasus technology grabbed headlines when it was used to hack Amazon founder and owner Jeff Bezos's phone, monitor Saudi dissidents, and surveil Mexican lawyers, UK-based human rights activists, and Moroccan journalists. The public took note. Public pressure forced Juliette Kayyem—a former Obama administration official, Harvard professor, and senior advisor to the NSO Group—to resign from her position with the spyware company and cancel a webinar on female journalist safety she planned to hold at Harvard. Public pressure also recently convinced IBM, Amazon, and Microsoft to temporarily stop selling facial recognition software to law enforcement because of evidence of these technologies' racial and gender biases and their use in the tracking and deportation of immigrants. Such social action against prominent companies engaged in dubious practices, and the academics and experts working for them, is still the rare exception. But it can and should happen more often if we want to redirect our efforts toward better AI.

The Mountains Ahead

ALAS, I HAVE TO END this essay not with a tone of cautious optimism, but by identifying some formidable challenges that lie ahead. The type of transformation I'm calling for would be difficult at the best of times. But several factors are complicating the situation even further.

For one thing democratic oversight and changes in societal norms are key for turning around the direction of AI research. But as AI technologies and other social trends weaken democracy, we may find ourselves trapped in a vicious circle. We need a rejuvenation of democracy to get out of our current predicament, but our democracy and tradition of civic action are already impaired and wounded. Another important factor, as I have already mentioned, is that the current pandemic may have significantly accelerated the trend toward greater automation and distrust in democratic institutions.

Finally, and perhaps most important, the international dimension deepens the challenge. Suppose, despite all of the difficulties ahead, there is a U.S. democratic awakening and a consensus emerges around redirecting AI. Even then hundreds of thousands of researchers in China and other countries can still pursue surveillance and military applications of AI technology and eagerly continue the trend toward automation. Could the United States ignore this international context and set the future direction of AI on its own? Probably not. Any redirection of AI therefore needs to be founded on at least a modicum of international coordination. Unfortunately, the weakening of democratic governance has made international cooperation harder and international organizations even more toothless than they were before.

None of this detracts from the main message of this essay: the direction of the future of AI and the future health of our economy and democracy are in our hands. We can and must act. But it would be naïve to underestimate the enormous challenges we face.

A WORLD WITH LESS WORK

Daniel Susskind

DARON ACEMOGLU URGES US to take the threat of automation very seriously, as both an economic and a political challenge.

On the economic front this might sound familiar, but until fairly recently many in the economics profession would have dismissed this view as misguided and alarmist. Indeed, before the turn of the century, the most widely used model of the labor market implied that technological progress could not possibly make workers worse off (though some might benefit less than others). Acemoglu rightly recognizes that AI is not suddenly going to make all humans redundant, even though it will likely make *some* humans redundant. And in my view, this fact is rooted in the imbalances that are already unfolding. Automation, Acemoglu writes, has acted as "the handmaiden of inequality." I would go further. The labor market is the main mechanism we use to share out income in society. Growing economic inequality reflects the existing problems with this arrangement: some workers get far more than others. Technological unemployment is simply a more extreme version of that same story—when some receive nothing at all.

Yet the challenges posed by AI, as Acemoglu argues, are not simply economic: they are also political. Acemoglu focuses on the threats to democracy and liberty. Again, I would go further. Politics is not simply about the hustle of politicians and the decision-making of the state. Nor is it simply about our freedoms (or lack thereof). It is also about *social justice*. This omission matters because many of the most troubling technological developments sit in this domain of our political lives: the online passport system in New Zealand that rejected the photograph of an Asian man because it concluded his eyes were closed, for instance, or online tagging systems that label photos of Black people as "apes" and concentration camps as "sport" and "jungle gym." These technological injustices must command our attention as well.

What is to be done? For the challenges that most concern him, Acemoglu argues that we can choose to shape our future—by using a variety of interventions to redirect AI development toward "a more productive path." It is revealing, however, what interventions don't make the cut. "Building shared prosperity predominantly on redistribution," he writes, "is a fantasy."

This is a striking declaration. For the only world where we would need redistribution to serve as the *predominant* mechanism for sharing prosperity is one where *most* people have to rely on redistribution for an income. But Acemoglu blew that strawman away in his opening lines: AI is not going to make most human beings redundant. What about the more likely world where a sizeable minority—say 15 or 20 percent—find themselves without work? *That* world is not a fantasy. Could redistribution work then?

The question matters because Acemoglu himself recognizes the "formidable challenges" involved in pursuing his alternative path away from excessive automation. This "type of transformation," he worries in closing, "would be difficult at the best of times." Should this realism not inform our response? Consider Acemoglu's own analogy with climate change. We now recognize that our response must involve both mitigation (through the reduction of emissions) *and* adaptation (to inevitably higher temperatures). But the response Acemoglu sketches to the challenge of automation amounts to mitigation alone. In the spirit of Acemoglu's own concerns, should we not also consider a world where we come up short, where our best efforts to redirect AI are defeated by the relentless advance of technological progress? I fear we are not yet taking that proposition—and its consequences—seriously enough.

One indication of the problem is a critical, implicit assumption about the nature of work running through Acemoglu's essay. It surfaces with the suggestion that unless we create "meaningful employment" for most people, they will lack a "viable social purpose." This assumption, I suspect, partly explains Acemoglu's resistance to that idea of adapting to a world with less work. On his view—widely held by others—the labor market is not only the preferred way to share prosperity in society, but the only serious way to share meaning and purpose as well. Put differently, technological change threatens to hollow out not only the labor market but also the sense of purpose that many people have in their lives.

A lot turns on whether you think this assumption about work and meaning is true. Whichever way you come down, though, taking the threat of automation seriously will require us to explore a wider array of policy possibilities than Acemoglu considers.

Suppose, on the one hand, you are unwilling to abandon the assumption that work and meaning are necessarily and exclusively linked. In that case everyone who is willing and able to work ought to be able to do so. But to make that happen will require very different interventions than the ones in Acemoglu's essay. If the labor market is unable to provide sufficient work, in spite of tinkerings with taxes and regulation, then we may need the state to provide meaningful employment in its place. In that case a job guarantee is not as radical as it might sound. Already today seven of the ten largest employers in the world are state institutions, and many of those in jobs involving tasks that are hardest to automate—nurses, carers, social workers—are employed by the state.

On the other hand, suppose you are skeptical of the conflation of work and meaning. Today, for instance, the majority of workers do not appear to gain a sense of purpose from their paid work: in the United States, a majority of workers report being either "not engaged" in their work (53 percent) or "actively disengaged" from it (13 percent), and only about 50 percent say they get a sense of identify from their job. You might also look at the 15 million people who actively volunteer in the United Kingdom—about half the total number of paid employees—and see that people can and do seek meaning outside paid work. In this case you might feel more comfortable with the prospect of decoupling work and income for some, instead providing them material support through redistribution while at the same time helping them find purpose through other socially valuable activities—even if those activities might not receive a traditional wage in the labor market.

For some these may be unfamiliar and uncomfortable ideas. They raise difficult questions, not only about economics, but about politics too. How would we pay for such a scheme? And how do we maintain social solidarity in such a world? But if Acemoglu is right about the magnitude of the challenge, then we need to make sure we are being bold in questioning our inherited assumptions and time-honored beliefs, and sufficiently imaginative in thinking about how we might be compelled to respond.

CENTERING WORKERS' POWER AND RIGHTS
Andrea Dehlendorf & Ryan Gerety

DARON ACEMOGLU IS RIGHT that the future is not inevitable: AI developments reflect economic and political decisions that we have the power to change. But the problems go beyond the abstractions of democracy and liberty. Largely missing from his essay is an awareness of the way these developments affect the day-to-day lives of workers in a highly unequal and racialized society. Any program of redirection must put these concerns front and center—and make workers' rights a nonnegotiable priority.

The markers of inequality are everywhere. Corporations invest in technology to reduce workers' share in profits, and as working people struggle, the wealthy respond by prioritizing investments in security, policing, and militarization. As a result, we see expensive and unnecessary technological advances that are primarily designed for control, punishment, and profit extraction: face recognition, worker surveillance, smart borders, just-in-time scheduling, predictive policing, risk assessments, and automated worker discipline. The use of technology to enforce social control, particularly against Black and brown people, has a long and violent history in the United States. For workers this history goes back to slavery and the plantation and was then formalized in the practices of so-called scientific management, which established control over a worker's every move.

People working in low-wage jobs confront these technologies in every facet of their lives. Today these workers face continuous monitoring and discipline on the job, only to return to a neighborhoods under constant police surveillance. They try to piece together a living wage with just-in-time scheduling or gig work, but when they inevitably fail and try to access public benefits, they are subjected to faulty fraud detection algorithms. Meanwhile immigrant workers subjected to technologically enforced work quotas must also confront surveillance by the Department of Homeland Security.

The system is relentless and crushing. Just listen to how one worker puts it. "In this country they are willing to do anything to ensure Black people don't lead a joyful, fruitful life," Courtenay Brown, an Amazon associate and leader of United for Respect, told one of us in a recent interview. "If they can't put you in prison, they are going to lock you away in a workplace that treats you as if you are. The system wasn't built for us—it was meant to control us. This is another means to keep us trapped."

This brutal reality is normalized through a dangerous and persistent narrative that weaponizes race. Mainstream media reinforces and amplifies this story, using all-too-familiar racist tropes. Low-wage workers are lazy and lack the skills for better pay; people experiencing poverty steal, making the rest of society unsafe—and when people turn to social benefits, they cheat. Almost always, here in the United States, the workers in this story are people of color.

The wealthy and powerful use these narratives to craft public policy that meets their need for low-cost labor and low taxes. The result is a punishing, untenable reality for all working-class people—Black and brown people bearing the overwhelming brunt.

Without strong labor protections and labor organizations, corporations use new technologies to systematically extract maximum value and profit from workers. These high-tech, low-road tactics include scaling up on-demand and just-in-time labor models to decrease wages and offset risk; deskilling jobs to lower wages and decrease the cost of high turnover; and worker surveillance and automated management to increase the pace of work. While the resulting job loss and deskilling are important, the harms are not abstract: this is a staggerly inhumane model that maximizes daily degradation, instability, and exhaustion.

Walmart—the world's largest company by revenue—was an early pioneer in utilizing centralized scheduling algorithms to match work schedules to peak customer hours, ensuring that workers did not cross the hours threshold that would make them eligible for full-time benefits. In 2017 the company began introducing robots to monitor inventory but rolled back that expansion last year. (Some analysts suspected that Walmart found it cheaper to use low-cost labor.) As the multinational corporation expanded during the pandemic, it doubled down on the use of cheap, temporary labor by leveraging lower paid, temporary Instacart workers. And while Walmart has experimented with this technology, staffing levels in many places have plummeted, adding stress and strain to already overworked and underpaid workers.

Nowhere is the punitive potential of technology more glaring than at Amazon, the world's second largest retailer. Warehouse workers are under constant pressure to meet draconian productivity quotas (called their "rate") and minimize their "time off task." Every minute is tracked, and every task is timed. A scanner tells workers exactly where to go, gives them mere seconds to get there, and then orders them to the next task. If a worker takes longer than the time they are given, that time is added to their time off task. At the end of the day, if their rate falls below an arbitrary threshold, they are disciplined and eventually fired. This constant surveillance causes workers stress, anxiety, and depression.

Beyond their inhumane forms of labor extraction, these practices also introduce other social costs. Amazon's injury rate is double the industry average, and a recent study found that 75 percent of workers were injured as a result of trying to make rate. In newer warehouses, where robots enforce a faster pace and demand repetitive motion, injuries are even higher. This state of affairs contributes to a high turnover rate, with the costs of unemployment offloaded onto workers' families and the public. During the pandemic Amazon also announced its vast network of warehouse cameras would be upgraded and used to detect social distancing. Instead of using the technology to protect workers, Amazon immediately began disciplining them for distancing violations.

On top of all this, these technologies directly undermine the ability of workers to speak out and to organize. Amazon and Whole Foods have both used intelligence analysts to monitor social media accounts of their army of low-wage workers and impede unionizing efforts. And as COVID-19 raged through warehouses, Amazon used rate, time off task, and social distance monitoring to find reasons to discipline workers who spoke out about health and safety conditions.

WORKERS HAVE DEMANDED an end to these punitive practices, and we should stand with them. Unless we act to stop ballooning corporate power, these punishing labor practices will become the norm.

How should we rewrite the rules? Workplaces themselves should be sites of democratic decision-making. After all, workers are the closest to the problems, and they know what works. While some of these technologies are new, the underlying, exploitative labor practices have existed for decades—corporate employers are simply accelerating them through technology.

We thus face an important choice. We can establish worker power and worker rights in the workplace to upend predatory models, or we risk accelerating an economic system that undermines all working people, concentrates wealth, and compounds the racial inequalities that were integral to the founding of this country.

We need policies that establish robust worker rights for the twenty-first century. To start we can make permanent the Essential Workers Bill of Rights, establish a task force of workers to guide pandemic recovery and our future economy, ensure stable schedules and access to full-time hours, and crucially, when it comes to the advance of AI, establish worker technology rights.

As long as our country prioritizes investment in security and enables exploitative business models, our technologies will mirror those incentives. We must rewrite the rules of the economy to incentivize good jobs, defund policing and militarization, force corporations to pay their fair share, and invest economic gains for a healthier future. Without these structural changes, no amount of AI ethics or corporate good will reverse the current trends.

The authors thank Seeta Peña Gangadharan and Mariah Montgomery for feedback and Ayele Hunt, Sheheryar Kaoosji, Brian Callaci, Strea Sanchez, Courtenay Brown, Aiha Nguyen, and Gabrielle Rejouis for contributing to our thinking.

Dehlendorf & Gerety

THE PANDEMIC BOLSTERED SUPPORT FOR NECESSARY REFORMS

Molly Kinder

DARON ACEMOGLU MAKES a convincing case for how AI can, and should, be redirected to create good jobs and invest in human potential. I agree with his core critique and analysis. But his essay misses the broader context of an even bigger disruption to work: the current COVID-19 pandemic and recession. Paving the way for a more equitable present and future of work will require addressing not only the various threats of automation but also the interrelated challenges created by the pandemic.

I have long shared Acemoglu's concerns about the potential for technological change to exacerbate inequality. My own research has raised concerns that AI, automation, and digitization may disproportionately impact those who are already financially insecure and displace the work of women, low-wage workers, and workers of color.

Despite these real concerns, it was an unexpected virus—not an algorithm or robots—that blindsided the world last year and caused staggering job losses among marginalized workers. The K-shaped pandemic recession has pummeled low-wage workers. Black and brown workers have suffered the worst losses, and women have left the labor force in droves—prompting the moniker "she-cession." The potential labor impact of new technologies, including AI and robotics, could undermine recovery efforts in the years ahead and exacerbate the challenges of job quality and quantity facing the most marginalized.

Building on Acemoglu's three-pronged approach, I would emphasize three priorities to address these interrelated issues: job creation, labor policy reform and institutional support, and worker empowerment in the workplace.

Job Creation

JOB CREATION IS PARAMOUNT. The pandemic has shifted the nature of the challenges facing American workers. Pre-pandemic the greatest challenge was a crisis of job *quality*. In 2019 my colleagues Martha Ross and Nicole Bateman calculated that more than 53 million people—44 percent of the U.S. workforce—received low wages. Technology and automation contributed to this quality crisis: many higher quality, middle-wage jobs were automated away, while poorer quality low-wage jobs in the service sector proliferated.

Now workers at the bottom end of the wage spectrum face twin crises of both job quality and job *quantity*. The pandemic has created a deep hole in the labor market, with 10 million people unemployed, compared to 5.7 million just before the pandemic began. While unemployment levels should drop significantly as the pandemic recedes and the economy recovers, millions of unemployed and low-wage workers will still struggle to connect to work—and especially decent work. New estimates from the McKinsey Global Institute project predict steady declines in low- and modest-wage jobs over the next decade, while new estimates from the U.S. Bureau of Labor Statistics predict either a decline or significant slowing in the growth of low-wage jobs through 2029. Automation and AI are just two factors in this decline. Job growth will also be hampered by lingering or even permanent shifts post-pandemic, including an increase in remote work, reduced business travel, some continued aversion to close physical proximity, shifts in customer habits, and an increase in online shopping. Combined with the potential for an upsurge in automation, these pandemic shifts will likely reduce the number of people working as cashiers, servers, retail associates, hostesses, receptionists, and clerical and administrative assistants. Many of these at-risk jobs are held by women.

While discussions of technological displacement often lead to a focus on retraining and skills, the primary challenge facing workers today is a *demand* problem, not a *supply* problem. An effective public policy response requires robust monitory and fiscal policies. The $1.9 trillion economic stimulus plan passed in early March 2021 is an important start, providing much-needed relief to families, employers, and state and local governments. An infrastructure bill could open additional opportunities to create jobs, including new clean energy jobs. The government could also subsidize employment directly, such as through community-oriented employment, an expanded national service program, and a youth employment program.

Labor Policy Reform

BEYOND JOB CREATION a second key priority should be strengthening labor market institutions and policy reforms. These steps are critical to improving job quality and curbing inequality, especially as better-quality middle-wage jobs continue to be automated. Acemoglu's essay touches on policy changes such as raising the minimum wage, but their centrality to a more equitable future of work cannot be overstated. The pandemic has spotlighted the enormous gap between the value that low-wage frontline and essential workers bring to society and the paltry pay they receive. My research with Laura Stateler found that upward of half of all frontline essential workers are in occupations that earn less than a living wage. Nonwhite workers make up a disproportionate share of the essential workers risking the most on the COVID-19 frontline for low wages. From security guards to home health aides, hospital housekeepers, warehouse workers, and grocery clerks, low-wage frontline jobs offer meaning and purpose but far too little pay, scant benefits, and little security.

The sacrifices of frontline essential workers during the pandemic have stirred society's conscience and buoyed support for policy change to better compensate them. Support for raising the federal minimum wage has grown, especially among Republicans and independents. Though Democrats in Congress did not succeed in raising the federal minimum wage to $15 hourly in the COVID-19 relief bill, the Biden administration and Democratic leaders in Congress have expressed strong support for continuing to push for a higher minimum wage. This federal effort is important: research that my colleagues and I conducted suggests wage increases are unlikely without government intervention. In an analysis of the pandemic profits and pandemic pay of thirteen of the largest retail companies, Laura Stateler, Julia Du, and I found that despite earning an additional $17.7 billion in the first three quarters of 2020 compared to 2019—a 42 percent average increase—most companies shared little of their profits with their workers through temporary pay bumps or permanent wage increases.

Worker Empowerment

A FINAL PRIORITY should be implementing new forms of worker voice and power in the workplace. Workers need a say in the decisions their employers make in deploying technology. Acemoglu's essay focuses mainly on democratizing AI *research*, but the decisions that employers make when they deploy these technologies in the workplace also matter. In many cases the technology is itself neither inherently good nor bad. What matters is how employers deploy it—and whether they involve workers in the process.

The status quo for workers is deeply concerning. In interviews we led at New America, Amanda Lenhart and I heard from dozens of workers that they had little say in the technologies their employers deployed. Cashiers, fast food workers, and clerical staff in jobs at high risk of automation often expressed feeling like they were a cost their employers were trying to minimize while aiming to maximize profit. They were especially resentful of self-checkout lanes (as Acemoglu has written about in other contexts) and other poorly designed technologies that made work harder for them. Most workers we interviewed were deeply pessimistic about the future for humans in their workplaces as AI, mobile ordering, online shopping, self-checkout, food delivery, and software innovations changed their work.

With union membership at historically low levels, workers have few formal avenues for having a voice in the workplace. The aggressive steps Amazon is taking to fight a groundbreaking union effort in Bessemer, Alabama, illustrate the challenges workers face as they seek a seat at the table as work is transformed. While the obstacles to collective bargaining remain formidable, politics and public opinion are starting to shift. President Biden recently issued a rare statement from the executive in support of the right of Amazon workers to organize, while the White House gave its support to labor legislation that would dramatically strengthen collective bargaining rights.

PROGRESS ON THESE three priorities is both necessary and urgent, but there are signs of hope. The unequal suffering and sacrifices caused by the pandemic have bolstered public support for structural reforms that could ultimately help redirect AI. A majority of Americans back a $15 per hour minimum wage, while 65 percent of Americans now support unions—the highest level since 2003. Still there are mountains ahead, including securing support from some Republicans in Congress. Until we meet this challenge, the future of work risks leaving many workers behind.

TECHNOLOGY-FOCUSED SOLUTIONS WON'T WORK

Aaron Benanav

ARE ROBOTS COMING for our jobs? Despite years of talk about a looming automation apocalypse, today it is clear that even the most advanced forms of AI cannot do most of the things humans can do. And the culprit isn't a lack of processing power; the technology itself is fundamentally limited.

Daron Acemoglu's intervention is part of a welcome new wave of automation thinking, more sober and clear-headed about how AI will transform work. But just because the story is less catastrophic doesn't make it optimistic. Though Acemoglu doesn't think new technologies will render *all* human labor redundant, he still sees a bleak feature unless we redirect the course of technological development—through greater public involvement in research and more democratic accountability. I agree that something needs to be done to solve our jobs crisis, but I think Acemoglu overstates the degree to which technology is responsible. As a result, the technology-focused solutions he offers are unlikely to lead to either shared prosperity or more satisfying jobs. What we really need is to rethink the connection between employment and economic growth.

Consider first what Acemoglu's argument gets wrong. To find out what threatens work today, he looks to the golden age of postwar capitalism, when economic growth "was not only rapid but also broadly shared." He notes the role played by minimum wage laws, collective bargaining agreements, and legal job protections in achieving this shared growth but also argues, correctly, that this policy framework wasn't the whole story. The key ingredient, for Acemoglu, was a particular pattern of technological change: back then technologies enhanced workers' productivity rather than automating their jobs away.

But is automation really responsible for the sharp decline in shared prosperity since the 1970s? Acemoglu's account makes it seem as if every middle manager's dream were coming true—firing tricky-to-manage humans en masse to replace them with robots, even if it saves little money. Yet if that were right and happening on a large scale, we would see evidence of it in labor productivity statistics. In a roboticized economy, each additional worker might contribute less to production, but since fewer workers would be involved in producing the same quantity of goods and services, average labor productivity—output per worker hour—would rise rapidly.

This isn't what we see. In fact the 2010s—which featured endless Silicon Valley boasting about advanced industrial robotics and AI—were actually the *worst* decade for average labor productivity growth since World War II. In manufacturing, output per hour worked grew at an annual pace of 0.6 percent between 2010 and 2019—glacial compared to 3.1 percent between 1950 and 1973. Labor displacement is certainly taking place to some degree in *some* firms. But it is unfolding in fewer firms than in the past and at a slower rate.

The same slowdown registers in other statistics as well. Contrary to what many readers might expect, the last decade saw extremely *low* rates of job churn—the rate at which workers change occupations over time—compared to earlier decades. That's yet more evidence that an army of robots is not pushing workers out of good occupations into bad ones. Global numbers also help to put our job crisis in perspective. The South Korean, German, and Japanese economies use many more industrial robots per manufacturing worker than the U.S. economy does, while at the same time employing much higher shares of their workforces in manufacturing. Robots help firms in those countries stay competitive in international markets and keep workers in their industrial jobs.

The problem we face in the United States is not too much pressure to change occupations brought on by automation, but rather too few opportunities to leave a bad job for a better one. Many workers, even highly educated ones, find themselves stuck in bad jobs, often laboring alongside other workers doing the same kinds of work for better pay. Think of adjunct lecturers, performing the same sort of labor as tenured professors for lower wages. Similar developments have caused wage disparities to rise within many occupations. Workers languishing in low-quality positions can't find anything better, exacerbating their already weak bargaining power.

Together these trends cast doubt on Acemoglu's thesis about the role of technology in creating shared prosperity. A clue to the real culprit lies in the fact that the end of the era of shared growth also saw a sharp slowdown in growth rates. The crisis we face today isn't caused by an automation-driven reduction in new jobs per unit of growth; the problem is that our growth-oriented economy is growing more slowly, generating fewer jobs as a result. And because working-class households are plagued by higher levels of underemployment, they are seeing fewer gains of the little growth that does exist.

This slowdown in growth isn't a distinctly U.S. phenomenon. It's a global trend, the result of the incredible expansion of world-wide industrial production capacities since World War II. Facing falling rates of return in hypercompetitive markets, industrial firms reduced investment in high-productivity activities. That shift, in turn, accelerated a trend in labor markets that was already underway: workers ended up taking jobs in characteristically low-productivity activities in the service sector. (There is no indication that AI is about to boost average service-sector productivity levels, and we should remember that similar claims about the rise of computers turned out to be false.)

One solution is to try to bring back the jobs lost to slower growth, but that strategy hasn't worked. As growth rates fell—keeping un-employment rates high—policymakers did everything they could to encourage firms to expand production. Governments lowered tax rates, issued public debt, deregulated the economy, and rescinded labor protections. None of these measures succeeded: growth rates stagnated, all while creating endless hardship for workers. Instead of a surge in private investment, the United States got two financial bubbles—first the dot-com bubble in the late 1990s, then the housing bubble in the mid 2000s—each followed by a further fall in economic growth. COVID-19 is now likely to reduce growth rates even more.

Future efforts to induce private investment are just as unlikely to succeed—as are technology-focused efforts like the ones Acemoglu recommends. Under conditions of slowing economic growth and widespread underemployment, publicly funded AI research will do little to solve the jobs problem. Nothing about the internet, touch-screens, or GPS—all developed with public research—implied the creation of Uber, which uses these innovations to prey on insecure people looking for scraps of work. Many companies will continue to find ways to intensify insecurity in order to better control and exploit workers.

So what can we do? In stagnating economies we need a fundamentally different economic engine—one that does not rely on economic growth to generate social stability. We need a new vision for public investment—undertaken not as a way to stoke private investment, but for the broad social benefits it creates. Crucial to that new paradigm of public investment will be rejecting technocratic forms of governance. Rather than supporting individual and community autonomy and a shared sense of purpose, states have tried to run the economy by remote control, centralizing decision-making in the hands of technocratic elites. We need public investment for and by the people, instead. We need democratically designed public protocols for the allocation of productive resources. Digital technologies may help, but the main obstacles that stand in our way are social, not technological, in nature.

DECOLONIZING AI

Shakir Mohamed, William S. Isaac,
& Marie-Therese Png

IT IS OFTEN ASSUMED that modern technologies will lift all boats. But like many other aspects of society, the benefits and opportunities of technologies such as AI are rarely shared equally. The myth of the rising tide can also conceal a troublesome undercurrent: while the benefits of new technology accelerate economic gains and provide everyday for the established, the harms of that same technology fall overwhelmingly on the most vulnerable and already marginalized. We agree with Daron Acemoglu that AI must be redirected to promote shared prosperity, but any genuine effort toward that goal will have to reckon with injustice—and work to ensure that both the risks and the benefits of new technology are shared equally.

Central to this work must be what we call Decolonial AI. The harms that have been documented as a consequence of AI deployments across the world—whether in facial recognition, predictive policing, resource distribution, shifts in labor practice, or health care diagnostics—did not emerge by chance. They result from long-term, systematic mistreatment and inadequate legal and economic protections rooted in the colonial project. Formal colonialism may have ended, but its logics, institutions, and practices endure—including within AI development and deployment. Any pathway to shared prosperity will have to contend with this legacy, and in particular with at least three distinct forms of algorithmic harm: algorithmic oppression, algorithmic exploitation, and algorithmic dispossession.

Algorithmic oppression describes the unjust privileging of one social group at the expense of others, maintained through automated, data-driven, and predictive systems. From facial recognition to predictive policing, such systems are often based on unrepresentative datasets and reflect historical social injustices in the data used to develop them. And amidst the COVID-19 pandemic, unrepresentative datasets have meant biased resource allocation, and prediction models further exacerbated health inequalities already disproportionately borne by underserved populations. Much of the current discussion about "algorithmic bias" centers on this first category of harm, but we must broaden our sight to other forms of algorithmic coloniality as well.

Whereas the harms of algorithmic oppression manifest during the deployment or production phase of AI, algorithmic exploitation and dispossession emerge during the research and design phase. Exploitation is perhaps clearest within the realm of workers' rights. The large volumes of data required to train AI systems are annotated by human experts—so-called "ghost workers," as Mary L. Gray and Siddharth Suri put it in their 2019 book *Ghost Work*. These jobs are increasingly outsourced to jurisdictions with limited labor laws and workers' rights, rendering them invisible to researchers and fields of study that rely on them. Algorithmic exploitation construes people as automated machines, obscuring their rights, protections, and access to recourse—erasing the respect due to all people.

But even these two categories—oppression and exploitation—do not exhaust the range of algorithmic harms. There is also dispossession: at its core the centralization of power, assets, and rights in the hands of a minority. In the algorithmic context, this can manifest in technologies that curtail or prevent certain forms of expression, communication, and identity (such as content moderation that flag queer slang as offensive) or through institutions that shape regulatory policy. Similar dispossession dynamics exist in climate policy, which has been largely shaped by the environmental agendas of the Global North—the primary beneficiary of centuries of climate-altering economic policies. The same pattern holds for AI ethics guidance, despite the technology's global reach. We must ask *who* regulatory norms and standards are designed to protect—and who is empowered to enforce them.

While these forms of algorithmic coloniality pose a significant obstacle to shared prosperity, we believe steps can be taken to achieve a more just future for AI. We should think of these efforts as *realigning* the course of modern technology, interconnecting us all as stakeholders.

To start we must think critically about what form of prosperity we seek to realign. Acemoglu's central argument relies on the collective distribution of increased economic productivity. However, given the inequalities in contemporary modes of production, should economic productivity be the measure of collective prosperity? While this form of prosperity, centering on material and economic well-being is an important element, a more comprehensive definition of prosperity should also encapsulate the fundamental role of dignity, greater expansion of rights and open society, and new forms of vibrant social and political community.

Second, like Acemoglu, we believe it is critical for AI researchers and practitioners to become more aware of the social implications of their work. Our approach to Decolonial AI describes this effort as creating a new *critical technical practice of AI*, achieved by developing a reflexive or critical approach to research. We are already seeing this type of shift at institutional levels. Several large AI research conferences, for example, now require researchers to include statements considering the potential impacts of their work.

But consciousness raising alone is insufficient. It is also crucial to advance participatory methods in research, development, and deployment—practices that incorporate affected communities into the process. This form of *reverse tutelage*, which facilitates reciprocal learning between practitioners and communities, aims to provide additional context—that researchers may not be in a position to appreciate—and refine the ultimate design of a given technology.

Recently there has been a surge of interest in advancing the new field of "participatory machine learning," which merges the practice of participatory action research with machine learning methods. While the work is promising, we must heed concerns that the concept of "participation" may do little work if it is not made precise and taken seriously. In particular we should distinguish between approaches that genuinely empower communities from those that merely repackage existing forms of data work—such as annotation or labeling—under the guise of participation. The industry has a crucial role to play in reforming and reimagining AI development and deployment, and it will need to actively rebalance these risks and benefits to ensure that social and economic gains benefit all stakeholders involved.

Last we must also pursue more systemic change beyond the AI industry itself. Further accountability can be established by building infrastructure for greater public awareness and scrutiny of AI applications. Better documentation and impact assessments for AI systems, which describe their intended usage and limitations on reuse and portability, could provide greater transparency and resources for impacted stakeholders to understand their potential harms and benefits. On the development side, there should be greater efforts to ensure higher standards for data collection and annotation, as well as more robust platforms for safe auditing or evaluation of AI systems and datasets by external stakeholders. As systems increase in scale and capability, we will also need greater investment into research on the sociotechnical factors concerning AI. And we must develop new frameworks to deepen AI ethics principles and their relation to human and civil rights law.

Algorithmic coloniality presents a daunting challenge, but it is not insurmountable. If we take these steps to realize the real promise of this technology, we can realign AI to serve the interests of us all.

THE PROBLEM IS WAGES, NOT JOBS
Erik Brynjolfsson

AS AN ECONOMIST my own research agenda is based on the premise that guiding AI toward beneficial outcomes is the most important issue facing our generation. Since Daron Acemoglu and I are kindred thinkers about this subject, I will take this opportunity to underscore and extend his essential message.

Acemoglu is right on three key points. First, core AI technologies are indeed advancing rapidly and becoming increasingly powerful. Improvements in machine learning, in particular—such as the deep learning techniques that made such rapid progress on the Imagenet dataset—are affecting more and more of the economy. In the right applications, the payoff can be large. Adoption is still in its early days—only 1.3 percent of firms in the United States have adopted robotics, for instance—but the numbers are growing rapidly. Second, the societal implications of AI are profound, especially regarding the future of work and our individual freedoms and democracy. Third, and most important, outcomes are not preordained.

This last point is not to be taken for granted. The most common question I get from audiences when I speak about AI is some version of: What will AI do to society? But this is not the right question to ask; it erases our agency. Acemoglu deserves special credit not simply for diagnosing the challenges created by these technologies, but also for suggesting a set of specific solutions. (In fact Acemoglu has long been one of the most powerful and rigorous advocates of the idea that we can and should direct the course of technical change. He published an influential article making this argument nearly twenty years ago.)

Regarding Acemoglu's diagnosis, I would emphasize the following details. When it comes to AI's effect on the workforce, the real challenge is wages, not jobs. While employment has grown over the past forty years, real wages for Americans with a high school education or less have fallen. Tyler Cowen and others have argued that this is evidence of a lack of technological progress, but overall GDP and GDP per capita have also grown, and 2019 saw a record number of billionaires. Drawing on the work of Acemoglu as well as David Autor, Lawrence Katz, Melissa Kearney, Frank Levy, and Richard Murnane, Andrew McAfee and I have made the case that advances in technology were not inconsistent with falling wages for some or even large part of the workforce.

The scale of these changes, and the bigger ones yet to come, is massive. The value of all the human capital in the United States—the sum of American workers' skills, experience, education, and know-how—is likely around $240 trillion. That implies that if our decisions change the trajectory of technology's effects on the U.S. economy enough to cause even a 10 percent change in that value, it would be worth more than an entire year's GDP (currently $21 trillion).

Brynjolfsson

As for AI's effect on democracy, we ought to be concerned about increasing polarization and enabling Orwellian levels of surveillance. As Marshall van Alstyne and I have written, it is precisely because digital technologies better enable us to find content and people we like that they can also separate and polarize us. These technologies can also massively amplify the power of the state to monitor the words and actions of its citizens, giving it the power to not only silence critics but even shape their thoughts. The implications are increasingly recognized by world leaders; as even Vladimir Putin has put it, "Whoever becomes the leader in this sphere will become the ruler of the world." In the wrong hands, the result may be what Jean Tirole calls a digital dystopia.

But no outcome is inevitable. We have the ability to direct AI, just as we can direct other types of technical change. Let me focus on three groups that can and should play a role in shaping AI for good: technologists, managers, and policymakers.

"It is remarkable," Acemoglu writes, "how much of AI research still focuses on applications that automate jobs." This is an under-rated problem. While it can be profitable to automate jobs, thereby substituting technology for human labor, in the longterm the bigger gains come from complementing humans and making it possible to create value in new ways. Moreover, when technology substitutes for labor, pitting humans against machines, it tends to drive down wages and lead to a greater concentration of wealth.

By contrast, when technology complements labor, wages tend to rise, creating more broadly shared prosperity. (In addition to substituting or complement labor, Tom Mitchell and I describe four additional considerations for how technology will affect wages: price elasticity, income elasticity, labor supply elasticity, and business process redesign. In many cases the net result of these six factors will be higher wages.) That is why McAfee and I have argued that "in medicine, law, finance, retailing, manufacturing, and even scientific discovery, the key to winning the race is not to compete against machines but to compete with machines." Indeed, at a major AI conference three years ago, I directly called on the gathered technologists to redirect their work from replicating and automating human labor to augmenting it.

Fortunately, a growing number of researchers are working to use AI to augment humans rather than replace them. Take Cresta, an AI start-up I advise. While many competitors work to develop fully automated chatbots that directly interact with potential customers, Cresta keeps a person in the loop. The system works alongside human operators, looking for opportunities to suggest ways of improving the dialogue—suggesting a product upgrade or service, offering a reminder about pricing, or coaching on tone and tactics. Via a series of A/B tests, Cresta found that this approach created demonstrable benefits for customers and also seems to benefit newer and less skilled workers especially, helping to close the wage gap and reduce inequality.

Managers, entrepreneurs, worker representatives, and other business leaders also have a critical role to play. Like technologists, they too often look at existing processes and ask the easy question: How can machines do what humans are now doing? The harder but ultimately more valuable question is different: How can technology and people work together to create novel sources of value? The more powerful and general the technology, the more important it is to rethink work. As Paul David, Warren Devine, Jr., and others have documented, significant productivity gains from electricity in manufacturing did not arise until managers fundamentally reinvented the organization of factories, a process that took thirty or more years—long enough for a generation of managers to retire and be replaced by fresher thinking. Likewise, modern enterprises are subject to similar dynamics, creating a lull in productivity while intangible investments in organizational and human capital are created complementing the new technologies like AI.

Policymakers can help each of the first two groups make better decisions by changing incentives. Take taxation. A key lesson from public finance is that we tend to get less of whatever we tax more. The current U.S. tax regime treats capital more favorably than labor. If two entrepreneurs each has a billion-dollar idea for using AI, the one who employs more labor will likely be taxed more than the one who is more capital-intensive. To the extent that labor income is more widely distributed, this element of our tax system discourages shared prosperity. This is a powerful argument for leveling the playing field. In fact there is also a good argument that we should go further to the extent we think there are positive externalities to employment. (Robert Putnam's 2015 book *Our Kids: The American Dream in Crisis* describes the negative effects of joblessness, while Anne Case and Angus Deaton's 2020 study *Deaths of Despair and the Future of Capitalism* documents rising deaths from suicide, drug abuse, and alcoholism in demographic groups most negatively affected by falling labor demand.) Depending on how strong these externalities are, they could reverse the classic results suggesting that taxes on capital should be lower than taxes on labor.

This list of change makers is not exhaustive, of course. Economists also have a role to play in guiding the debate, as does the public at large. As the power of AI grows, our values become increasingly important. It's incumbent on each of us to think deeply about what kind of society we want. Bringing these issues to the forefront of popular discussion is crucial.

In the face of all these possibilities for change, I remain a mindful optimist. Acemoglu notes that we are far from consensus about how to make progress. While this is a challenge, it is also an opportunity to forge a shared vision. But our window is short. If wealth and power become increasingly concentrated, and if democracy is further weakened, we will reach a point of no return. We can and must act now to prevent that from happening—and to redirect AI for the good of the many, not just the few.

Brynjolfsson

BEYOND THE AUTOMATION-ONLY APPROACH

Lama Nachman

DARON ACEMOGLU HIGHLIGHTS the worrisome direction of AI development today—replacing jobs, increasing inequality, and weakening democracy. But he concludes by emphasizing that "the direction of AI development is not preordained." I agree—and one way we must "modify our approach" is to think of AI less as a substitution for human work and more as a supplement to it.

The current narrative about AI puts it in competition with humans; we need to think instead about the possibilities—even the necessity—of human and AI collaboration. AI tends to perform well on tasks that require broad analysis and pattern recognition of massive data, whereas people excel, among other things, at learning from very limited data, transferring their knowledge easily to new domains, and making real-time decisions in complex and ambiguous settings.

Over the last decade, deep learning has shown great improvements in accuracy in many areas—including visual recognition of objects and people, speech recognition, natural language understanding, and recommendation systems—due to an explosion in data and computational power. As such, businesses across all sectors are trying to exploit AI and deep learning to improve efficiencies and productivity. This typically leads to automation of limited and repetitive tasks instead of looking holistically at the complete workflow, going beyond what is easy to automate, and figuring out how to solve the problem differently.

The automation-only approach indeed has its limits. First, such solutions tend to be fragile and don't adapt well to specific environments or changes in tasks over time. Second, these solutions, trained on large datasets, often encounter cases they were not trained for, resulting in many failures. Current approaches focus on adding more data to the training, resulting in exponential growth of models and training requirements. In fact one study on the computational efficiency of deep learning training showed that since 2012, the amount of computation used in the largest training runs has been increasing exponentially at a staggering rate, doubling roughly every 3.4 months. Finally, automation-only approaches tend to produce black boxes, without insights for users on how to interpret or evaluate their decisions or inferences—further limiting their usefulness.

What if we thought about work more holistically, as a collaboration of human and AI capabilities? In their 2018 *Harvard Business Review* study "Human + Machine: Reimagining Work in the Age of AI," H. James Wilson and Paul Daugherty report that their research on 1,500 companies in 12 domains showed that performance improvement from AI deployments increased proportionally with the number of collaboration principles adopted. (The 5 principles studied included reimagining business processes, embracing experimentation/ employee involvement, actively directing AI strategy, responsibly collecting data, and redesigning work to incorporate AI and cultivate related employee skills.) This improvement is not surprising when we consider the complementary nature of human and AI capabilities: people can train, explain, and help to sustain the AI system and ensure accountability, while AI can amplify certain cognitive strengths, interact with customers on routine tasks, help direct trickier issues to humans, and execute certain mechanical skills via robotics.

Systems that leverage the strengths of both can deliver compelling, efficient, and sustainable solutions in overall task performance, in training the AI system, in training people—or all of the above. But creating collaborative systems poses unique challenges we must invest in solving. These systems need to be designed to perceive, understand, and predict human actions and intentions, and to communicate interactively with humans. They need to be understandable and predictable—and to learn from and with users in the context of their deployed environments, in the midst of limited and noisy data.

Consider manufacturing. While automation is changing the way we build factories, we still rely on humans in many tasks—especially in troubleshooting, machine repair, system configuration optimization, and decision-making. If an AI system can aid engineers and technicians in performing these tasks and making decisions—if it can observe and recognize their activities, understand the context, bring them relevant information in the moment, and highlight anomalies and discrepancies—people can make better decisions, reduce deviations, and fix errors sooner. In addition systems that collaborate with many users can recognize and draw attention to similarities and differences in human behavior, thus facilitating human learning across group of people who might have never worked together.

The AI system, in turn, can evolve over time with the user's help. When a task changes, or procedures are modified, it can rely on the user's input to modify its understanding, capture relevant examples, and retrain itself to adapt to the new setting. For this approach to work, the system needs certain capabilities. First, it needs to be able to observe users, infer their state robustly, and predict their intentions and actions—even their level of engagement and emotional state. Second, the system needs to communicate efficiently with users around a shared understanding of the physical world. People do this all the time when they work together; they refer to objects, gesture and point to resolve ambiguity, predict and anticipate future actions, and proactively intervene when necessary. We need to go beyond our current chat bots to multimodal, contextually aware, interactive systems. Third, the collaborative system needs to learn from users incrementally, constantly adjusting its perception and decision-making based on users' input. It needs to have a principled understanding of its uncertainty and seek more data to improve its learning and explain its actions.

While achieving these capabilities might seem daunting, the payoffs will extend well beyond manufacturing. For example, research in education shows the high potential for human/AI collaboration to improve learning outcomes. Pedagogical research suggests student engagement and personalization result in better learning outcomes. Collaborative systems have the potential to help teachers understand the unique needs of every student and personalize their learning experience. Or, as in the kind of remote learning situations we are experiencing in the COVID-19 pandemic, AI systems might work with students as they perform different tasks, assisting them and providing insights to the teachers to help them address students' different needs. This is even more critical in early childhood education. But, as in the case of manufacturing, these systems need to be able to understand the students actions, communicate with them in the context of their shared physical environment, and learn from the students and the teachers over time to develop robust capabilities. There are similar opportunities for AI systems with these capabilities, in elder care, in support for people with disabilities, and in health care.

If we want to change the prevailing narrative from human/AI competition to human/AI collaboration, we will no doubt face challenging design issues—as well as serious privacy and safety challenges. But success would mean higher value, more scalable and adaptive solutions, and better societal outcomes in the long run.

BETWEEN DYSTOPIA AND UTOPIA
Kate Crawford

THE PANDEMIC has dramatically increased the profits and power of the technology sector. Many people turned to video calls, delivery services, and home devices to keep life and work afloat, to the great benefit of the largest tech companies. And while some expect to see an increase in workplace automation due to lockdowns and widespread infections, in some cases the reverse has happened: Amazon alone hired 500,000 new workers in a single year.

Does this mean that we should not fear a future of automation, inequity, and job loss that Daron Acemoglu warns us about? On the contrary, it means that the greatest threats might already be here, depending on who you are. The nature of work has changed for many; there is profound concentration of power in just a few companies; and after decades of neoliberalism and racist policies, democratic safeguards have been materially weakened.

A central tenet of Acemoglu's argument is that AI is driving ubiquitous labor automation, to the point where there will not be enough tasks for humans to perform. He argues that industry priorities should shift so that AI complements humans, and workers can take on more complexity, where technologies empower them to adapt and learn. The types of automation we have seen to date have more commonly done the opposite, where algorithms determine the speed at which work is done, and laborers are unable to predict when their shifts occur because they are set "flexibly" to benefit the corporation. While the elimination of entire job categories is one risk of automation, another is the creation of workplaces with increasingly extreme asymmetries of power between workers and employers. Already, many people work while monitored by apps, "nudged" to meet company targets, and ranked in real time. Some would call this AI complementing human work—but having "humans in the loop" does little to address the loss of agency, autonomy, or creativity in these contexts. The negative impacts of AI on human labor can far exceed the statistical job losses that are directly accountable to automation.

The automation debate, which occurs all along the political spectrum, swings between dystopian and utopian visions of the future. In one account automation will wipe out entire job categories and leave millions unemployed—the "robots are taking our jobs" thesis. At the other extreme, radical automation is welcomed as a way to create a post-work, post-scarcity society (or "fully automated luxury communism," to use Aaron Bastani's term). Less attention is paid to the *current* experiences of AI-modulated workplaces, particularly for those in low-wage work who currently experience increased surveillance, algorithmic assessment, and strict modulation of time. Acemoglu, while closer to the dystopian end of labor automation, hopes that AI can augment and support workers rather than replace them. He cites the potential for AI to empower teachers to adapt their materials in real time, or for blue-collar workers to collaborate with robotics technology. But we should ask who negotiates the terms of these collaborations, and if teachers and factory workers will have any choice but to accept them. In reality automation is largely presented to workers as an ultimatum, a forced collaboration driven by a vision of efficiency defined by scale and statistical optimization.

Many forms of work are becoming shrouded in the term "artificial intelligence," hiding the fact that people are often performing rote tasks to shore up the illusion that machines can do the work. Already millions of people are needed to prop up supposedly automated services: tagging, correcting, evaluating, and editing AI systems to make them appear seamless. Others lift packages, drive for ride-hailing apps, and deliver food. Rather than representing a radical shift from established forms of work, the encroachment of AI into the workplace should properly be understood as a return to older practices of industrial labor exploitation that were well established at the turn of the twentieth century. That was a time when factory labor was already "augmented" with machines and work tasks were increasingly subdivided and tracked. Indeed, the current expansion of labor automation continues the broader historical dynamics inherent in industrial capitalism. A crucial difference is that employers can now use AI to observe, assess, and modulate the work cycle and bodily data—down to the last micromovement—in ways that were previously off-limits to them.

Consider Amazon's fulfillment centers, a workplace where humans and robots collaborate. When writing *Atlas of AI*, I spent time in Amazon's center in Robbinsville, New Jersey, a major distribution node for the Northeast. I watched the robotic ballet of orange Kiva robots moving across the floor, locking onto programmatic pathways, carrying trays of goods to be sorted by humans. But the experience of the workers in the warehouse looked far less serene. The anxiety of making the "picking rate"— the number of items they must select and pack within the allocated time—takes a clear toll. Many of the workers I encountered wore compression bandages: knee supports, elbow braces, and wrist guards. Others skipped meals and bathroom breaks to keep up with the rate.

Amazon is the second largest U.S. employer, but humans in these augmented workplaces can appear more like vestigial limbs. They complete the specific, fiddly tasks that robots could not: the necessary connective tissue to get ordered items into containers and trucks and delivered to consumers. People still have jobs, but each job is a compilation of small, banal tasks not easily allocated to robotic efforts. Amazon provides a canonical example of how a microphysics of power—disciplining bodies and their movement through space— is connected to a macrophysics of power, the logistics of planetary time and information, designed to maximize profits at a global scale.

If we want to understand how AI and automation will change the nature of work, we need to understand the past and present experience of workers as they become part of these systems. Current workplace AI largely remixes the classical techniques used to increase the granularity of tracking, nudging, and assessment such as in Henry Ford's factories and Samuel Bentham's inspection houses, with hints of Charles Babbage's theories of time management, and Frederick Winslow Taylor's micromanagement of human bodies. From the lineage of the mechanized factory, the tech industry has developed a model of work that values increased conformity, standardization, and interoperability—for products, processes, and humans alike.

Acemoglu believes that with changing research priorities and sufficient democratic oversight, labor automation and surveillance can be tamed.

He suggests one solution is for AI researchers to be more aware of and vocal about the social consequences of their work, but this overlooks the hundreds of AI researchers that have been pointing to the problems of workplace surveillance, automating social services, discrimination, racialized and gendered logics in AI, privacy harms, and labor exploitation. Research is important but not sufficient, as commercial directives are set elsewhere. The uncomfortable truth is that to change the current trajectory of AI development will require changing the structures of power in big tech, from corporate priorities to government regulation, from who owns AI infrastructures to how AI systems are conceptualized, built, and deployed.

As we recently witnessed in the showdown between Facebook and the Australian government over its media bargaining laws, some companies won't hesitate to switch off their services if regulations threaten to interfere directly with their ways of doing business. The key lesson is that no single law or intervention will be enough to address large-scale systems of labor exploitation and infrastructural power. Here too history can be instructive. Improvements in work conditions over the last century came from collective movements, where workers from different industries came together to win victories like workplace safety, weekends, and the eight-hour workday. Powerful business interests and neoliberal governments chipped away at labor rights and regulations over the past thirty years, but there are signs of progress across the tech landscape. The recent move by Amazon workers to unionize in Alabama has galvanized many into new collective calls for change, in the hope that there are ways to reduce the asymmetries of power in the already automated present. But this won't be easy: the last century has shown that the response of powerful industries has been to grudgingly accept change at the margins but to leave untouched the underlying logics of production.

THE FRONTIER OF AI SCIENCE SHOULD BE IN UNIVERSITIES

Rob Reich

THOUGH AI HAS SEEN powerful advances over the last decade, the state of the art falls far short of artificial *general* intelligence—the Holy Grail for some technologists, and a voguish fear for many observers. But the systems we do have are already powerful enough to send tremors through our individual, professional, and political lives, and astounding advances in language and vision models in just the past few years portend only more seismic activity to come. Daron Acemoglu reminds us that the effects of technological innovation are not preordained, and he provides an essential playbook for citizens in democratic societies to steer the development of AI in a direction that supports rather than subverts human and societal flourishing.

I agree with Acemoglu that such redirection is essential. But I want to point to two neglected dimensions of his analysis: the transformation of the workplace, and the essential role of government funding and policy in making academia rather than industry the center of research activity.

AI threatens more than the elimination of human labor by machines or autonomous systems; it is also transforming the experience of the workplace, often for the worse. Most of the discussion about the social and economic effects of AI and autonomous systems has focused on the technological displacement of human labor—the rising number of job-destroying robots. This discussion is essential, but such a focus obscures an equally important debate about how autonomous systems change the experience of work. It comes in at least three forms.

First, service-industry employers—one of the largest sectors of the economy—once provided stable and predictable work schedules, with employers absorbing the risk of potential labor oversupply in the face of weak demand. Now automated systems help drive optimal staffing schedules, generating uncertain work hours and total compensation and shifting the risks to employees.

Second, where once the supervisor on the shop floor monitored employees for being on-task and productive, the rise of AI-driven "bossware" creates a surveillance panopticon of eyeball tracking, keystroke logging, location tracing, and other forms of automated monitoring of labor. Less invasive but increasingly common tools in the workplace, such as Slack and video conferencing, expose even the most ordinary forms of collaboration to surveillance.

And third, AI-driven systems also sit behind the platform or gig economy, connecting customers to providers of services—think TaskRabbit, Uber, Lyft, and DoorDash—who are not full employees but contractors. These platforms provide the benefit of flexible work schedules to the gig worker but also deny the ordinary protections of full employment, from health care to retirement benefits. Once again risk to the owners of staffing with full-time employees is shifted to the worker, creating new forms of precarity.

The upshot is that policy responses to AI, as Acemoglu rightly says, must rely on more than redistribution. But we must also go beyond redressing the distortionary incentives in the form of asymmetrical tax rates on labor versus equipment and software. The ongoing shifting of risk from employers to workers and the privacy-abusing practices of bossware also require policy invention.

This conclusion leads to the more general question posed by Acemoglu: How can government policy steer the development of AI away from automation that has negative consequences for individuals and societies? His three-pronged approach of removing policy distortions, changing research norms, and rejuvenating democratic governance is spot-on. But I would point to a number of different policy areas that could yield clear progress toward the aim of an AI future that generates shared prosperity, enhances the livelihood of workers, and increases our freedoms.

One worrisome trend at the frontier of AI science is the brain drain of talent from academia to industry. The most recent AI Index reports that in North America, 65 percent of graduating PhDs in AI went into industry in 2019, compared to 44.4 percent in 2010. The result is a steady rise in research coming from industry—research that quite possibly responds more to corporate and profit-making interests than the goal of individual and societal flourishing. The reason for the brain drain is not (just) the ordinary explanation that AI talent is scarce and industry compensation far exceeds what academia can pay. Another factor is the greater access to computing power and enormous pools of data, especially in big tech companies. In many cases research at the frontier of AI science cannot be carried

Reich

out from within academia—at least without massive funding and corporate partners to provide data and computers.

This problem can be addressed through policy by the obvious mechanism of greatly increasing federal AI science budgets that flow to universities. The federal government can also fund the creation of a national research cloud that provides computers and data access to a wide array of academic researchers. The newly formed Institute for Human-Centered AI at Stanford, where I serve as associate director, is championing this idea. The institute itself might be a model for other innovations that can shape the development of AI for the better—gathering together scholars from across the entirety of the university, training the next generation of AI scientists as well as policymakers, and reaching out to industry, civil society, and government to convene and educate. To take stock of the social transformations wrought by AI, we need research far beyond the precincts of computer science departments.

Still better, we need to move beyond the study of AI's effects in the world only after new technology has already been created and deployed. We can change the norms of AI science by bringing talent from across the university into AI labs, as it were, changing the frontier of research into an interdisciplinary collaboration. In this spirit, though universities will never be able to match the compensation packages offered to AI talent by industry, they do offer settings for research and collaboration with scholars across fields and professional schools that few companies, if any, can match. The emerging study of AI ethics provides just one example. The experience of leading scholars such as Timnit Gebru at Google provides a cautionary tale for the fate of interdisciplinary research that runs afoul of corporate control. Universities provide academic freedom; companies do not.

Learning to govern AI before it governs us is one of the most important tasks of the twenty-first century. Leaving the task to AI scientists alone, especially to those who answer to corporate leaders rather than academic norms fully apart from the marketplace, is a trend we must reverse.

Reich

THE MEANS OF PREDICTION
Rediet Abebe & Maximilian Kasy

DARON ACEMOGLU CONSIDERS the social impact of AI through two pathways: the consequences for labor and wages, and the effect of social media and surveillance technologies on democracy and individual freedoms. He argues that these twin challenges lead to a worrisome and mutually reinforcing dynamic, but also that the future is not doomed. The direction of technical change is not a given—it is a consequence of policy choices and social norms that remain within our power to change.

We could not agree more. In fact many of the arguments Acemoglu makes regarding the impact of AI on the labor market could be made regarding any impactful new technology, from steam engines to electrification. Such technologies substitute for some forms of labor, complement others, and have generally led to a redistribution of employment and incomes. And as history has revealed, their development, use, and impact is indeed not preordained; it has changed over time in response to political and social choices.

All this is true for AI as well. In this spirit we want to spell out further how we might redirect the development of AI, focusing on issues that arise specifically in applications of AI. In particular we want to call attention to the limitations of two approaches to achieving algorithmic justice.

A salient—and often distressing—use of AI involves targeted treatment of individuals in a wide range of domains, from hiring and credit scoring, to pricing, housing, advertisements, and our social media feeds. These applications have elicited criticisms about fairness and discrimination by algorithmic decision-making systems.

But these criticisms stop far too short. Many leading notions of algorithmic fairness—often defined as the absence of discrimination between individuals with the same "merit" within a given modeling context—may in fact have the effect of justifying and preserving the status quo of economic and social inequalities. They take as given the decision-maker's objective as a normative goal and do little to challenge the profit-maximizing objectives of technology companies. Discrimination is then effectively defined as a deviation from profit maximization. In our work we have argued that such notions of fairness suffer from three crucial limitations.

First, they fail to grapple with questions about how we define merit (such as trustworthiness, recidivism, or future education success) and evade questions about whether it is acceptable to generate and perpetuate inequality justified by this notion. Because of this improvements in the predictive ability of algorithms can increase inequality while reducing "unfairness."

Second, these fairness definitions are narrowly bracketed: they only consider differential treatment within the algorithm. They do not aim to compensate for preexisting inequalities in the wider population, nor do they consider inequalities they may generate within the wider population. Unequal treatment that compensates preexisting inequalities, such as affirmative action in college admissions, might reduce overall inequality in the population. But such unequal treatment would be considered "unfair" according to standard definitions.

Third, leading notions of fairness consider differences between protected groups (e.g., people of different genders) and not within these groups (e.g., differences between women of different races, socioeconomic backgrounds, immigration and disability status, among other axes of oppression). But as intersectional feminist scholars have long argued, equal treatment across groups can be consistent with significant inequality within groups.

Instead of this fairness-focused framework, we think the study of the impact of algorithmic decision-making on society calls for an inequality- and power-based framework. Our work has shown that decisions that increase fairness, as it is commonly construed, can in fact lead to greater inequality and decrease welfare. This tension brings a crucial question into sharp relief: Do we want fairness, as defined by narrow notions of what constitutes fair allocation or treatment, or do we want equality?

Given these limitations of a fairness-based approach to AI redirection, we need to think more deeply about who controls data and algorithms. How do we reason about the impact of algorithmic decision-making on the overall population? At their core AI systems are just systems that maximize some objective. But who gets to define the objective? Whose goals count? That is very much a function of the property rights assigned by society. As Marx might have put it, we need to ask who controls the means of prediction.

The flip side of this question of property rights is who we consider to be a possible agent of change when it comes to redirecting the course of AI development and deployment. Just as there is a question about who gets to pick the objectives that AI systems aim to maximize, there is a question about who might potentially remedy the adverse social impact of these technologies.

A booming field in academia and beyond considers the ethics of AI, focusing on questions such as fairness, accountability, and privacy. Whether explicitly or implicitly, much of this field takes as its audience the corporations implementing these technologies, or the engineers working for these corporations. We believe that this focus is misguided, or at the very least incomplete.

While social norms certainly matter for behavior, economic and financial forces ultimately determine organizational objectives in our capitalist economy. We must not lose sight of the fact that corporations will first and foremost maximize profits. There is a reason that "corporate social responsibility" goes "hand in hand" with marketing, as one Forbes contributor puts it, and that arguments for diversity are often advanced in terms of the "business case" for a more diverse workforce. Left to industry, ethical considerations will either remain purely cosmetic—a subgoal to the ultimate objective of profit maximization—or play only an instrumental role, whether because of the elusive business case for diversity, or as a way to avert antidiscrimination lawsuits, union organizing, bad press, consumer boycotts, or government regulation.

In order for these pressures to play a meaningful role in corporate calculations, we need external regulation, advocacy, and oversight: actors outside these corporations who are aware of the problems new technologies might be causing, who understand how they impact all members of society, and who can influence norms, change incentives, and take direct action to alter the course of development. There are many forms this action might take. There are organizations and unions of workers who have the potential leverage of strikes. There are civil society actors, nongovernmental organizations, and journalists who have the potential leverage of public attention and consumer boycotts. And there are government policymakers, the judiciary, regulatory agencies, and politicians who have the leverage of legislation and litigation. All these actors have an essential role to play in Acemoglu's vision for a more just future for AI. We cannot leave the decisions to the companies themselves.

We thus want to conclude with a call to arms. Those of us who work on the ethics and social impact of AI and related technologies should think hard about who our audience is and whose interests we want to serve. We agree with Acemoglu that the future is not preordained. But his program for redirection will succeed only if it includes a wider range of agents of change—especially those who have been left to the margins of society and bear a disproportionate brunt of the burden of algorithmic harms.

IT IS NOT TOO LATE
Daron Acemoglu

I AM GRATEFUL to the respondents for these thoughtful replies. I am particularly heartened by the broad agreement that the U.S. labor market, like that of other industrialized nations, is fundamentally not working—and that AI isn't helping. Beyond this consensus, however, there are many important nuances in these comments. It is impossible to do justice to all of them here, but they can be usefully separated into four groups.

The first is the most optimistic. Erik Brynjolfsson and Lama Nachman agree with the broad outlines of my critique of the current course of AI development, but they are more sanguine than others about the future—and about what is already going on in the industry. Particularly on point is Brynjolfsson's contention that "the real challenge is wages, not jobs." Nachman is right, too, when she emphasizes "the complementary nature of human and AI capabilities." One helpful example is Brynjolfsson's discussion of Cresta's work on chat bots. And as both point out, much more can be done when it comes for AI's opportunities to empower rather than replace humans.

Yet I do not see these technologies becoming central in the current environment without significant efforts at redirection. Automation and monitoring remain the main focus of AI development, and a few large companies with a strong focus on algorithmic automation are having an oversize impact on the direction of this technology. Consistent with this, my recent research with David Autor, Joe Hazell, and Pascual Restrepo suggests that a lot of current AI is in automation mode, rather than the more collaborative mode Brynjolfsson and Nachman envision. I hope time—and our efforts at redirection—will prove them right and me wrong.

THE NEXT TWO GROUPS think that things are worse than I have described. Daniel Susskind argues that a certain degree of job loss to automation is inevitable—and thus that technological change is less susceptible to redirection than I contend. In particular, in a version of John Maynard Keynes for the age of AI, Susskind foresees the labor market, at least for some workers, almost completely breaking down with "technological unemployment." Based on this assessment, he advocates "decoupling work and income" using schemes such as state-guaranteed jobs and more redistribution (perhaps as a universal basic income or a guaranteed basic income). Like Keynes he believes that such schemes are feasible in part because it is possible to help people "find purpose through other socially valuable activities."

Just as I hope Brynjolfsson and Nachman turn out to be right, I would be happy if Susskind's predictions about the decoupling of work and purpose are borne out. But even if such a separation were feasible in the long run, I think it would be imprudent to presume that a large fraction of the current (or perhaps even the next) generation will be able to adapt seamlessly to a workless future without losing social meaning—and in the process further degrading democracy and cohesion in our society.

A third group also believes things are worse than I have described, but for different reasons than Susskind. These authors agree that digital technologies and AI have played a major role in our predicament, but they also see other factors at work that are equally important.

Andrea Dehlendorf and Ryan Gerety emphasize the dwindling power of and protections for workers, even as they recognize that this is partly a technological story. They also rightly emphasize that new technologies disproportionately disempower minorities and women, especially in the service sector. Molly Kinder argues that COVID-19 has done much more damage to workers in one year than decades of excessive automation, and she too recognizes the unequal nature of the suffering. These are important observations, but I expect that some of the damage from COVID-19 will be reversed, while there is no turning back from jobs lost to automation.

Rob Reich points out two aspects to which I did not give enough emphasis. First, he joins Kate Crawford, as well as Dehlendorf and Gerety, in stressing the technological transformation of workplaces—constant monitoring, insecure staffing arrangements, the increasing disempowerment of workers in the gig economy. He also notes the troubling dominance of AI companies over academia, which I agree must be addressed.

All these respondents suggest policy remedies in line with my assessment: regulation of the technology sector, more diverse voices, and more power for workers have to be part of the solution.

I wholeheartedly endorse these prescriptions, but I would reiterate that such reforms, by themselves, won't be enough and may even backfire. Available evidence suggests that in current circumstances, greater wage pressure and collective bargaining power for workers may encourage even more automation by firms. Efforts to empower workers—in the workplace and in politics more broadly—must go hand-in-hand with efforts to redirect technological change.

Some of these objectives need robust regulation—a point underscored by Crawford and Reich, as well as by Rediet Abebe and Maximilian Kasy in their discussion of actors outside the AI industry. I should have been more emphatic on this point. But there was a reason for my focus on attitudes and norms: the policy prescriptions highlighted by these authors will not be effective without a change in social norms. Short of such changes, there will be myriad ways for tech companies to avoid or circumvent regulations, and they can do so without suffering sufficient blowback from their employees or customers to force them to change course (in the same way that, without pressure from their customers or employees, banks circumvented regulations before the financial crisis). I thus stand by my conclusion that the first step has to be securing a broad recognition of what current digital and AI technologies are doing to the labor market and democracy, and building general agreement about the responsibilities of the technologists and leading firms in this area.

Two responses—by Abebe and Kasy, and by Shakir Mohamed, Marie-Therese Png, and William S. Isaac—offer complementary analyses to mine, but like the others in this group, they again rightly emphasize the adverse effects on marginalized groups. Abebe and Kasy are undoubtedly correct that prevailing standards for algorithmic fairness fall short of ensuring an equitable distribution of costs and benefits of many AI applications founded on "targeted treatment." Mohamed, Png, and Isaac draw out similar concerns through the frame of "algorithmic coloniality"— algorithmic harms that grow out of the "colonial project."

Of course tensions related to inequality of social power and the role of businesses in steering the direction of technology are nothing new. Nonetheless the regulated market economy of the 1950s and '60s generated plenty of technologies that increased workers' productivity and earnings (and even some, like mass media, at times helped amplify organized labor's voice). However pernicious the practices and legacies of colonialism, to understand and to correct the problems that AI is creating specifically for labor and democracy, we should focus on changes since the 1970s—including the decimation of regulation, greater focus on shareholder values and cost-cutting, the dominance of the business and technology models of a few tech companies, the disappearance of government leadership in research, and increasing tax subsidies for automation.

THE COMMENT by Aaron Benanav is the most critical of my argument. Benanav shares my assessment of the current state of the labor market, but he takes a more skeptical view of "the degree to which technology is responsible." In his telling what we need is not a change in the direction of technological development but a more fundamental transformation of the economic system. He calls for "public investment for and by the people," based on "democratically designed, public protocols for the allocation of productive resources."

Yet it is not clear how to implement these prescriptions, and there are no clear models of past success in this realm. The swift and shared prosperity of postwar American and European economies wasn't based on large-scale public investments that sidelined market incentives (not even in the Nordic countries); it was driven by a regulated market economy generating rapid technological advances. My discussion of renewable energy was meant to provide a case in point. Massive public subsidies to clean energy could have been tried in the 1980s and early 1990s, but it would have been very, perhaps even prohibitively, expensive. The chief factors that redirected technological change in the energy sector— delivering impressive cost reductions for clean energy along the way— were some basic regulations, R&D inducements from the government, and nonpecuniary incentives provided by changing social norms. If we had followed Benanav's vision, we would be far behind where we are in terms of having a fighting chance against climate change.

The same lessons apply today for the future of AI. It is not too late to put technology to work to create jobs and opportunities and to support individual freedom and democracy. But doing so requires a massive redirection of technological change, especially in the field of AI. We cannot expect this redirection to be led by today's corporate giants, whose profit incentives and business models have centered on automation and monitoring. Nor can we expect anything better from China's state-led model, which has, if anything, been even more fixated on using technology to disempower workers and citizens. The only path out of our current predicament requires both robust regulation and a fundamental transformation in societal norms and priorities, so that we put pressure on corporations and governments as customers, employees, and voters—while we still can.

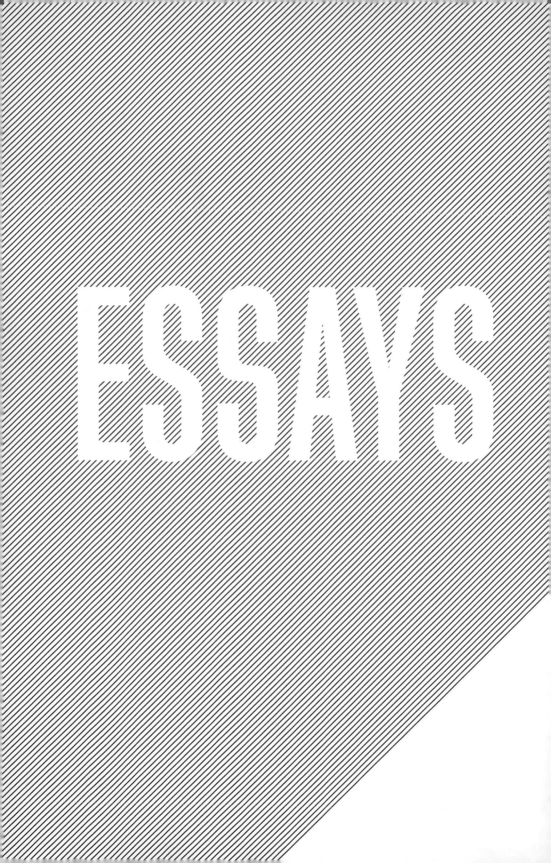

ESSAYS

STOP BUILDING BAD AI
Annette Zimmermann

AN AI-POWERED "facial assessment tool" compares your face to supposedly "objective" standards of beauty and offers an "aesthetics report" with recommendations for cosmetic surgery. Amazon's new Halo health band aspires to recognize emotions and warns women who wear it when their voice sounds too "dismissive" or "condescending." A tool used by Stanford University researchers uses facial recognition technology to predict whether you are gay.

Should these technologies exist? Whether AI can make accurate predictions in these areas is far from clear. But beyond this technical issue, we ought to ask whether we need such tools to begin with. Are the problems they set out to solve worth solving? How does predicting someone's sexual orientation, possibly without their knowledge and against their will, make the world better, or more just? What harms might result from the use of such a tool? We should ask questions about the goals and likely consequences of a particular technology before asking whether it could be made to work well. And when we do so, we need to be open to the possibility that some AI tools should not be built in the first place.

Unfortunately, these questions are not asked often enough about AI. One reason is economic: especially in the absence of robust legal regulation, ethical reflection takes a back seat to the profit motive. Another is cultural: an ongoing wave of renewed AI optimism, following the AI "winters" of the late 1970s and early '90s, often crowds out concerns about its potential harms. Then there is AI exceptionalism, the conceit that AI development is too important or distinctive to be stifled and thus should be exempt from the caution and regulation we apply to other technological innovations. Still another reason is philosophical: the assumption is that AI goes wrong only when it relies on biased data or when it fails to perform well.

Certainly AI can help us perform many important and complex tasks that humans cannot accomplish at the same scale and speed. Many AI projects are worth pursuing, and many developers have good intentions. But that does not license a general norm in favor of building and deploying any AI tool for any purpose, regardless of the social and political context in which it operates. Indeed, there are important reasons why we ought to challenge this presumption in some cases. A just future for AI demands that we think not just about profit or performance, but above all about purpose.

IN PRINCIPLE, there are two basic strategies we might pursue in order to mitigate the harms of a certain technology. On the one hand, we might try to optimize it, with the aim of making it more accurate, fairer, more transparent—better at doing what it is supposed to do. On the other hand, we might refuse to deploy or build it altogether—especially if we judge its goals or likely consequences to be ethically indefensible.

A powerful current within contemporary culture favors the former strategy. After all, who could object to making things better? In this view, there are many mechanisms available for improving flawed AI. We can alter algorithmic decision rules and improve datasets by making them more fine-grained and representative. We can better measure and operationalize key concepts relevant to the given task. We can test AI systems by simulating what would happen if we were to deploy them, and we can deploy them in relatively controlled, constrained ways before implementing them at scale—for instance, in sandboxed projects carried out by academic and industry research teams.

But it is important that we recognize this is not our only option. For tools that have already been deployed, we might choose to stop using them. Recent bans of law enforcement facial recognition tools in several U.S. cities illustrate this approach in action. San Francisco's recent ordinance concerning acquisitions of surveillance technology, for instance, argues as follows: "The propensity for facial recognition technology to endanger civil rights and civil liberties substantially outweighs its purported benefits, and the technology will exacerbate racial injustice and threaten our ability to live free of continuous government monitoring." Even private corporations agreed that non-deployment was the best solution in this case: Amazon, Microsoft, and IBM all voluntarily adopted non-deployment moratoria until facial recognition in policing is subject to top-down regulation. These moves may be motivated more by financial interest—the desire to avoid the costs of PR fallouts—than by ethical commitments. Still, it is noteworthy that even the industry's largest corporations have publicly advocated for non-deployment of technology that has already been built.

Non-deployment efforts in this area have been prompted by influential studies showing that currently used facial recognition systems are highly inaccurate for women and people of color. This is a good reason not to deploy these systems for now, but it is also important to recognize that the unregulated use of such systems might well be politically and morally objectionable even if those tools could be made highly accurate for everyone. Tools that support and accelerate the smooth functioning of ordinary policing practices do not seem to be the best we can do in our pursuit of social justice. In fact, the use and continued optimization of such tools may actively undermine social justice if they operate in a social setting that is itself systemically unjust.

There is one further option, of course. Carrying this logic even further back in the development process, we might decide not just to avoid *deploying* certain AI tools but to avoid building them altogether.

WHICH OF THESE STRATEGIES—optimize, do not deploy, or do not build in the first place—is best? It is impossible to say in general. Whether a particular AI tool warrants development and deployment will depend heavily on a large number of empirical factors: how the tool works, which problem it is tasked with solving, how the technology interacts with social structures already in place. These kinds of facts about the social world are subject to change. Political and institutional transformations may alter the way people are situated socially; evolving norms will affect the way people and institutions interact with technology; technology itself will dynamically reshape the society it is a part of. We thus should not hope for a generic ethical rule, a blanket endorsement one way or another.

Instead, we must develop nuanced, context-specific frameworks for thinking through these issues. This work will entail taking on several obstacles to more robust ethical and political reflection on the strategies at our disposal.

One is the cultural imperative, especially popular in the tech world, to move fast and break things—Facebook's infamous motto until 2014. Former Yahoo! CEO Marissa Mayer is often quoted as saying that "with data collection, 'the sooner the better' is always the best answer." Amazon's leadership principles feature similar language: "Speed matters in business. Many decisions and actions are reversible and do not need extensive study. We value calculated risk taking." In an environment that prioritizes speed above all else, technologists are less likely to ask why or whether a certain technology ought to be built than to think, *why not?*

At the same time, many practitioners are increasingly concerned about—and actively working to mitigate—the harms of AI.

Most major tech companies now have designated teams focusing on "ethical," "trustworthy," or "responsible" AI. But it is unclear whether corporations will empower such teams to intervene in the development and design of new technology. Google's recent firing of Timnit Gebru and Margaret Mitchell, co-leads of the company's Ethical AI team, shows that industry AI ethics efforts are often limited and outweighed by competing corporate goals.

Tech employees, for their part, are also increasingly organizing themselves—often against significant pushback—with the aim of holding their employers accountable. Consider the Alphabet Workers Union. "We will use our reclaimed power to control what we work on and how it is used," its mission statement reads. "We are responsible for the technology that we bring into the world, and recognize that its implications reach far beyond Alphabet." Such statements may be compatible with refusing to build or deploy new technology, but they typically lean heavily toward optimization—specifically, optimization within powerful corporations. "We will work with those affected by our technology to ensure that it serves the public good," the statement continues. "Alphabet can make money without doing evil," it says elsewhere on its website. But whether such justice-oriented optimization is compatible with the pursuit of profit—within a small number of powerful private corporations, to boot—remains to be seen.

A second obstacle we must reckon with is the contention that developing a potentially harmful technology is better than leaving it to bad actors. Many technologists reason, for example, that if *their* team does not build a given tool, someone else will—possibly with more sinister motives. On this view, arguments not to build or deploy may look like giving up, or even a way of making things worse. The Stanford researcher who used facial recognition technology for predicting sexual orientation, for example, argued that it would have been "morally wrong" not to publish his work:

> This is the inherent paradox of warning people against potentially dangerous technology. . . . I stumbled upon those results, and I was actually close to putting them in a drawer and not publishing—because I had a very good life without this paper being out. But then a colleague asked me if I would be able to look myself in the mirror if, one day, a company or a government deployed a similar technique to hurt people.

But this argument does not stand up to scrutiny. Nothing prevents a bad actor from repurposing knowledge and technological capabilities gained from an AI tool first developed by a well-intentioned researcher, of course. And even tools developed with good intentions can ultimately have damaging effects.

A third obstacle is a too limited conception of the ways AI can be harmful or unjust. In many familiar examples of algorithmic injustice, accuracy is distributed unequally across different demographic groups. Criminal recidivism risk prediction tools, for instance, have been shown to have significantly higher false positive rates for Black defendants than for white defendants. Such examples have elicited significant ethical reflection and controversy, helping to call attention to the risks of AI. But we must also recognize that AI tools can be unjust even if they do not rely on biased training data or suffer from disparate distributions of error rates across demographic groups.

Zimmermann

For one thing, even if developers are well intentioned, the *consequences* of implementing a particular algorithmic solution in a specific social context may be unjust, because algorithmic outputs reflect and exacerbate social biases and inequalities. It may also be that the *goal* of an AI tool is simply not just to begin with, regardless—or even indeed because of—the tool's accuracy. Consider Megvii, a Chinese company that used its facial recognition technology in collaboration with Huawei, the tech giant, to test a "Uighur alarm" tool designed to recognize the faces of members of the Uighur minority and alert the police. Here it is the very goal of the technology that fails to be morally legitimate. A related problem is that human decision-makers, prone to automation bias, may fail to scrutinize algorithmic classifications, taking ostensibly neutral and objective algorithmic outputs as a given instead of interrogating them critically. In still other cases, it may be the *logic* of the technology that is objectionable, leading to what philosophers call "expressive harm": the use of particular categories and classifications in AI tools can convey a demeaning, harmful message, which becomes unjust in light of prevalent social norms, assumptions, and experiences. Tools that attempt to deduce sexual orientation or other personality traits from one's physical appearance, for example, may contribute to reinforcing the harmful message not only that it is possible to "look like a criminal," or to "look gay," but also that it is valid to infer personal characteristics and future behavior from the way a person looks. The upshot of these various examples is that the potential harms of AI range far beyond datasets and error rates.

A final obstacle to more robust ethical reflection on AI development is the presumption that we always have the option of non-deployment. If at some point in the future it turns out that an AI tool is having unacceptably bad consequences, some might say, we can simply decide to stop using the tool *then*.

This may be true in some cases, but it is not clear why we should think it is always possible—especially without industry-wide regulation. The labor effects of automation, for example, may well be effectively irreversible. In current market conditions, it is hard to imagine how a company could take back its decision to replace a human-executed task with an AI-driven, automated process. Should the company face backlash over its AI tool, current incentives make it far likelier that it would seek to find another way to automate the task rather than rehire humans to execute it. The pressure to automate is now so strong in some sectors that some companies are *pretending* to have built and deployed AI. In 2016, for example, Bloomberg News reported that personal assistant startup X.ai was directing employees to simulate the work of AI chatbots, performing avalanches of mind-numbing, repetitive tasks such as generating auto-reply emails and scheduling appointments. It would be naïve to think that once such tools are actually built and deployed, the work force could easily revert to its pre-automated structure.

For another example of the limits of non-deployment, consider DukeMTMC, a dataset of two million video frames recorded in public spaces on Duke University's campus and made publicly available without protecting the identities of the people included in the videos. The data wound up being used for controversial research on computer vision-based surveillance technology, and it was taken down in June 2019 after significant public criticism. But as Princeton University researchers recently pointed out, at least 135 research papers utilized that dataset—and others derived from it—*after* it had been taken down. Non-deployment thus did not make the ethical and political risks associated with this technology disappear.

FOR ALL OF THESE REASONS, we must take the option not to build far more seriously than we do now. Doing so would not only help to make the development of AI more just. It would also lead us to reflect more deeply on the demands of justice more generally.

Return to the example of facial recognition tools used in law enforcement. Rather than trying to scale up and optimize existing policing practices by augmenting them via AI, we could instead ask: What would more just law enforcement look like? Which institutional, economic, and legal transformations are needed for this purpose? The answers to these kinds of questions may not necessarily involve AI—at least not before other sociopolitical changes are made first.

Making these judgments—deciding whether a particular AI system should be built and optimized, or not built or deployed at all—is a task for all of us. One-off non-deployment victories and shifting industry norms are important achievements, but they are not enough. We need systematic regulation and democratic oversight over AI development. We need new frameworks for both national and international governance on these issues. And we need meaningful opportunities to deliberate collectively about whether powerful new forms of technology promote, rather than undermine, social justice.

When asking these kinds of questions, we must resist the tendency to view AI in isolation from the larger history of technological development. Instead we should look for important parallels with the development and regulation of other powerful technologies, from nuclear weapons to gene editing.

As science and technology studies scholar Sheila Jasanoff observes in her 2016 book *The Ethics of Invention*, these urgent forms of engagement will require vigilant public action and continual democratic scrutiny. "Important perspectives that might favor caution or precaution," she notes, "tend to be shunted aside in what feels at times like a heedless rush toward the new." However, history shows that when it comes to technological development, the new is not always just. Getting clear on the purpose and value of AI is more important than the rush to build it or make it better.

WORKPLACE TRAINING IN THE AGE OF AI
Nichola Lowe

WE ARE OFTEN TOLD that Americans are facing a skill crisis—one that will intensify in the coming years with greater adoption of digital technologies and a learn to-code imperative. But this skill crisis is not due to inadequate educational systems or an unprepared generation of younger workers, as some would argue. The problem is that too few U.S. businesses share responsibility for skill development.

Many employers have been either unwilling or unable to invest sufficient resources into work-based learning and the creation of skill-rewarding career paths that extend economic opportunity to workers on the lowest rungs of the labor market. On the whole, U.S. businesses do invest more resources in workforce training than U.S. federal or state agencies. But a highly uneven pattern of investment threatens to intensify economic disparity: on average, larger firms are more generous and consistent with workforce training than are their smaller counterparts. What makes this training imbalance especially troubling is that smaller businesses make up the vast majority of employer firms in the United States. And until the downturn caused by COVID-19, their numbers had been rising, as larger firms—whether by choice or due to investor pressure—outsourced more functions to smaller suppliers or subcontractors.

Beyond firm size, there are other sources of training inequities that disproportionately affect low-wage workers. Paradoxically, most employers, regardless of size, limit support for skill development to employees who are already highly educated. The result is a bifurcated structure that further concentrates rewards at the top of the occupational hierarchy, with few opportunities for advancement reaching those at the bottom.

What are the economic consequences of this skills imbalance? What can be done to encourage employers—particularly smaller-sized firms—to accept greater responsibility for skill development? And how can organizations that strive to improve working conditions and extend economic opportunity lend a hand? I think an essential component to the solution is learning to see skill as a problem of employment rather than of education—and of building institutions to make that vision a reality.

TO ANCHOR THESE ISSUES, consider the case of Maddie Parlier, a woman from South Carolina profiled in a 2012 *Atlantic* essay by Adam Davidson. At the time, Maddie was a twenty-two-year-old single mother with only a high school degree, working an entry-level job at a small-sized automotive parts manufacturer. Her story sheds light on the "jobs crisis" facing the millions of low-income Americans trapped in dead-end, low-wage work—and often performing routine tasks that in the near future could easily be automated.

Common proposals to help workers like Maddie fall into three broad categories: higher education, minimum wage legislation, and workplace training and support. While education and wage legislation both have central roles to play in any policy program for workers, workplace training, we will see, is also essential—even though it receives far less attention as a policy goal.

Higher Education

ACCORDING TO DAVIDSON, Maddie's fate—and by extension, that of all low-income individuals—is sealed by not having a college education (an associate's degree or higher), that golden ticket into the middle class that remains out of reach for approximately half of the U.S. working-age population.

Prominent labor scholars and analysts have advanced proposals to address this problem. Some align closely with Davidson's central tenet—that Maddie's employment prospects will greatly improve if she quits her unfulfilling day job manufacturing specialized fuel injectors to instead pursue a college degree. As supporting evidence, Davidson offers the experience of Maddie's coworker, Luke, another ambitious young employee with an associate's degree in applied machining from a nearby community college. His degree not only guarantees Luke a better starting salary but also clears the path for occupational mobility and a higher, more secure position at the firm.

There are serious limits to this view of the problem, however. For one thing, there is the financial strain that often accompanies higher education. If Maddie left her job to pursue a degree, she would forgo her biweekly paycheck, making it harder to feed herself and her daughter and pay for childcare, rent, and other household essentials. Though federal education funding and welfare payments could provide some temporary relief, they are risky without certainty regarding eventual job prospects. Would a college degree guarantee good employment and open the door to the middle class? What about her age (including the added years out of the labor market)? Or her responsibilities as a single mother? Or her inability to relocate or commute long hours? Do these and other factors foreclose long-term economic security even with more education?

This supply-side approach also ignores a major driver of income inequality: the low quality of entry-level jobs. Though more education *might* help Maddie get a better job elsewhere, it leaves the quality of her own bad job untouched—ready for another economically vulnerable applicant to assume. Any proposal to improve Maddie's circumstances must improve the job itself, including changing how her contributions as a worker are recognized and rewarded.

Raising the Minimum Wage

AN ALTERNATIVE PROPOSAL IS LEGISLATION to raise Maddie's minimum wage. Raising wages would obviously ripple through the low-wage labor market, benefiting Maddie and other undervalued workers. Projections by the Economic Policy Institute, a progressive think tank, reinforce this point: an increase in the federal minimum wage to $10.10 per hour would benefit upward of 17 million low-wage workers in the United States. If the rate were set at $15 per hour, an additional 15 million workers would experience a sizable earnings bump. These numbers would fall if legislation were limited to the state or local level, but they demonstrate the wide net that active labor market policy casts.

There is thus little doubt that a minimum wage hike could increase Maddie's earnings potential. But could it also generate better career prospects for Maddie within the firm, allowing her to gain additional skills and higher wages? Scholars and activists who call for increased minimum and living wage standards contend that they would propel Maddie's employer to introduce productivity-enhancing measures to offset some of the additional labor cost, making better use of employees' underutilized talents. Whether this claim is right is a central question of the polarized debate over minimum wage legislation. Critics point out that Maddie's employer might respond to a higher minimum wage in a less inclusive and supportive manner—perhaps adopting cost-cutting measures that would ultimately cost Maddie her job.

Recent studies find little to no job loss from a mandated wage increase, however, suggesting our economy could easily accommodate a universal raise. Especially compelling is a set of "border" studies that pairs neighboring jurisdictions with similar economic and industry characteristics, with one adopting a higher minimum wage standard. This work shows that raising the minimum wage standard does not cause significant or precipitous declines in overall employment. Follow-up studies find that employers who add new jobs after a higher wage ordinance has gone into effect either pass the increased cost on to their clients or adopt cost-saving measures to offset the mandated wage hike. Raising wages is therefore a promising option that could help improve earnings for low-wage workers.

Still, in light of Maddie's precarious economic position, it is important to recognize that these results are simply averages. While a majority of employers in jurisdictions that have enacted higher wages continue to expand employment, others did not. Davidson's interview with Maddie's employer suggests that her boss was in the second camp: convinced that his small manufacturing company would struggle to absorb added labor costs, he was already pondering automation to replace entry-level workers. He is not alone. Interest in automation is growing. A recent study suggests that U.S. manufacturers may be particularly sensitive to higher minimum wages compared to their counterparts in place-bound service industries, such as retail and restaurants.

The upshot is that employers, even in manufacturing, can respond to higher wage requirements by shoring up entry-level jobs through upskilling workers or instead by replacing workers with technological alternatives. And this choice set highlights the limits of a blunt policy instrument, such as raising wages, in isolation. Backup action is needed to augment wage legislation. Reinforcing this point, scholars involved in pathbreaking minimum and living wage research recognize that higher wage standards are only a starting place—and that more work is needed to translate those wage gains into better job opportunities.

Workplace Training and Support

THIS BRINGS US TO A THIRD PROPOSITION: some combination of work-based change and institutional support.

Proposals in this vein include recommendations for job-site mentoring, meaning that frontline workers like Maddie would be paired with company engineers or product designers—including technical experts like her college-educated colleague Luke, who, according to Davidson, works separate from the entry-level workforce. Cross-functional mentoring allows for idea sharing and offers a channel for strengthening peer advocacy, such that higher-ranked workers could attest to the dependability and character of new coworkers and lobby for them to receive additional support and greater job security.

A related recommendation is for Maddie's employer to provide dedicated time for group problem-solving. This might involve employer-sponsored training: formal on-the-job structures augmented through off-site coursework. This option could easily be supported through a company-backed tuition reimbursement plan or a flexible work schedule that would enable Maddie to build on her foundational knowledge of high school math and science, subjects she enjoyed and excelled at as a student. Maddie's employer could even create a federally registered apprenticeship program, partnering with a neighboring community college to align on-the-job learning with a technically relevant associate's degree or industry-recognized vocational certificate.

These work-based learning opportunities could result in Maddie earning more as she develops new skills and give her the chance to move up the organizational ladder. We might even push the argument further and assume these workplace changes will result in an enduring employee–employer relationship that will simultaneously support higher productivity, process innovation, and career advancement—a win–win for Maddie and her employer.

Yet a closer look at the circumstances surrounding Maddie's employer suggests it would be hard-pressed to implement many of these changes on its own, especially in light of a hypercompetitive auto parts market flooded with low-priced products imported from China. This difficult reality leads back to Davidson's view: that social mobility is only possible if Maddie leaves her dead-end job to pursue a college degree. That is, unless we recognize the larger societal and economic inequities we create by letting firms off the hook for skill development, shifting too much of that burden to institutions of higher learning and the students they educate.

WHAT CAN BE DONE to redress this imbalance? We need a scalable solution that encourages employers to accept greater responsibility for skill development and to extend economic opportunity to workers on the lowest rungs of the U.S. labor market. Three principles help to map a course for institutional action.

The first involves situating skill development within a larger job quality framework. Skill development is not simply a precursor to accessing good jobs: it is what *makes* them good jobs. Quality employment gives workers access to learning opportunities and employer-sponsored training that can broaden career prospects, both within the firm and across associated industries. In this regard, training opportunities are not just a secondary consideration; they are as integral to job quality as high wages, comprehensive benefits, workplace autonomy, and job satisfaction.

Numerous writings have placed employer support for skill development on equal footing with family-supporting wages and other income-enhancing benefits. The International Labour Organization, an advocacy arm of the United Nations, has long associated skill development with "decent work." Many scholars have done the same. It is imperative that workforce and labor advocates better leverage the power of skill to push U.S. businesses to improve the quality of the jobs they offer.

To help illustrate this possibility, consider a second principle: that skill confers shared value on workers and employers. Skill is not something that workers alone cherish. It holds value for both employers and employees. Workers seek out new skills to advance their careers but also to make their daily work lives more fulfilling. Employers recognize skill as essential for enhanced productivity and advancing product and process innovation. (This is manifest in the number of employers who are concerned about industry skill shortages.) A better-skilled workforce is a resource for employers to respond to emergent or unanticipated economic and technological challenges. More than just offering a promising solution to rising income inequality, then, skill improvements extend options for industry innovation and create the conditions for broad-reaching economic resilience.

Still, while workers and employers might share a positive association with skill, they do not always interpret it in the same way—for numerous reasons. At the most basic level, what exactly *is* "skill"? Is it just technical competency, narrowly construed, or does it encompass less tangible forms of cognition, creativity, and social capacity? Moreover, *who* is deemed skilled—and who has the power to make that determination? Are skills owned by individual workers, or are they part of a collective, tightly woven into the social fabric of everyday work?

These considerations bring us to a third principle: skill is an ambiguous and malleable concept. This ambiguity arises from different perspectives, experiences, and pressures facing workers and employers. Sometimes the resulting uncertainty can work against efforts to improve skill development at work. It can magnify employers' fears that investments in on-the-job training will reward other firms if a newly trained worker accepts a job elsewhere. It can also create workplace friction that can undermine employers' attempts to further extend work-based learning. Many scholars and workforce practitioners are uncomfortable with this uncertainty, so they seek greater clarity and precision through better skills assessment and measurement.

By contrast, I argue that skill ambiguity is something we should embrace. Doing so can open the door for institutional action, allowing workforce advocates to cross the threshold into the firm and move employers through a skills-centered transformation to enhance the work experience of economically vulnerable workers and job seekers.

Indeed various types of worker-supporting institutions, from labor unions to workforce service providers, have used firm interest in skill as an opportunity to intervene at the firm level. They do so by building on the agreement among workers and employers that skill development is valuable for advancing economic opportunity and progress.

These institutions strengthen their worker advocacy role by harnessing—and sometimes heightening—uncertainty around skill. They can engage skill ambiguity to advance broader conceptions of expertise, advocating for lower-ranked workers who might otherwise be dismissed by their employers or coworkers as unskilled or under-qualified. They can push employers to reinterpret skill investment as critical to future business success rather than as a liability or risk. They can extend negotiations around skill to influence thornier aspects of employment relations, such as negotiations over higher wages and more extensive worker benefits. And they can link employer investments in workforce skill to critical choices in technology adoption, guiding employers to implement new and improved technologies to enhance job quality and grow the business, expanding rather than cutting overall jobs. Uncertainty around skill thus offers a powerful resource that institutional actors can use to align the interests of workers and employers.

HOW CAN WE LEVERAGE these principles to make much-needed change? A compelling model comes from workforce institutions that adopt a "dual-customer" approach, serving both job seekers and employers in order to enhance employment prospects through organizational expansion.

These institutions, commonly referred to as workforce intermediaries, are diverse in their institutional origins and affiliations. Some are outgrowths of community-based nonprofit organizations. Others are extensions of well-established labor unions. Still others are branches of a county- or state-funded community college system. Despite their various affiliations, all help firms deepen their commitment to skill development by formalizing internal structures that recognize and reward work-based learning and occupational mobility.

Workforce intermediaries also link firms—and their frontline workers—to educational institutions, especially community and vocational colleges, that offer customized training and technical assistance to firms, along with portable credentials for workers. But this institutional partnership represents much more than the typical supply-side push for job seekers to rack up more credentials or degrees; workforce intermediaries tap these educational partners as a means to strengthen their influence over employers and to build an external path to reinforce skill development opportunities within firms.

In partnering with educational institutions to utilize existing course offerings and training expertise, these intermediaries help reduce employer training costs. This means that firms can spend internal resources on supporting employees' career development through work-based learning. The result is a model that forges interdependencies between employers and educational institutions in order to create greater capacity to support skill development. Ultimately, an integrated institutional platform emerges that recognizes and reinforces skill development as a shared social responsibility.

We have many concrete case studies to learn from and build on. It is estimated that there are hundreds of workforce intermediaries in the United States—many more if we include new programs and initiatives embedded within publicly funded community colleges and high schools. While workforce intermediaries have long existed, their visibility increased in the early 1990s with a high-profile convening of progressive foundations, labor scholars, and practitioners. Since then, complementary efforts have been undertaken to expand the number of U.S. workforce intermediaries, aided by generous funding and support from philanthropic foundations and alliances—such as the Annie E. Casey Foundation, the Ford Foundation, and the National Fund for Workforce Solutions—as well as through such practitioner preparation programs as the Aspen Institute's Sector Skills Academy. A rich body of scholarship on workforce intermediation also provides inspiring examples through in-depth case studies, demonstrating employment and wage gains through rigorous experimental and quasi-experimental analysis.

These intermediaries are not without their challenges. In their idealized form, they would be well positioned to increase economic opportunities for low-income workers and job seekers by influencing employer decision-making in hiring, wage-setting, and advancement. In reality, many practitioners within these intermediaries acknowledge the difficulties of persuading employers to make changes to existing organizational structures. This has led some intermediaries to double down on their provision of social services, including pre-employment training, offering a bundle of supports to low-income individuals and creating a safety net should their attempts to secure well-paying jobs fail. While these intermediaries do direct job seekers to "high-road" employers who provide quality jobs, they often struggle to take their work a step further to transform "bad jobs into good."

Another challenge that prevents intermediaries from having greater impact is the dominant view that technological change renders certain skill sets worthless and obsolete. In this "skills mismatch" framing, institutions are expected to step in only after firms have chosen new technologies and implementation is already underway. Employers assume that these institutions will be on call, prepared to update and refine workforce skills in response to industry's adoption of new technology.

But it need not be this way. An alternative, more proactive and embedded approach is already in the works and yielding promising results, with far-reaching implications for entry-level and frontline workers. On the Las Vegas strip, the Culinary Workers Union engages its 57,000 casino-working members in an annual technology survey, elevating the visibility of worker knowledge in new technology development and deployment. A state-funded technology center in upstate New York has partnered with frontline manufacturing workers to codesign a collaborative robot or co-bot. Building trades unions in northern California are partners in Factory-OS, a state-of-the-art "prefab" construction facility, that combines pioneering robotics, in-house R&D, and advanced manufacturing methods. These unions help recruit and train the firms' workforce, also advocating for wider adoption of manufactured solutions to address the region's affordable housing crisis.

These examples and others show it is possible to intervene earlier in the innovation process, positioning workforce skill as critical to technological decision-making from the start rather than as an afterthought. With more robust forms of intermediation, employers can learn there is value to having frontline workers continually participate in technological decisions and development. By extension, proposed technological changes can be subject to focused advocacy, especially in support of workers whose skill sets might appear tangential to innovation. Advocates can challenge this myopic perspective on worker equity grounds but also help employers realize worker exclusion is detrimental to future business success.

This alternative vision rejects the idea that technological change is predetermined and inevitable, refusing to relegate workforce institutions to the back seat. Instead it foregrounds new institutional alliances to rebalance the politics of skill, with renewed political focus not just on strengthening worker negotiations in the workplace but also on anchoring those gains to a broader, shared vision of inclusive innovation. In this unfolding future, power is not held by technology (or technologists) but lies in how institutional agents help technology designers, developers, and users—including employers—engage frontline workers in processes of innovation, including a reinterpretation of technological choices. What is most critical is an open and shared process of discovery, with frontline workers centrally involved in shaping new technologies and their applications.

This intersection of inclusion and innovation offers an opportunity for new forms of labor advocacy—one that treats skill development and innovation as two sides of the same coin. As advocates forge these new institutional partnerships, they must reconcile older labor traditions that focused on labor processes internal to a firm with more recent social and labor movements that seek to build worker mobilization and political power. They also must push back against the ever-popular assumption—one too happily advanced by technology futurists, influencers, and financiers in Silicon Valley and other high-tech hubs—that technological changes are inherently disruptive to jobs and damaging for less educated workers.

More than a critique of technological hubris, we need this response to empower workforce institutions to elevate their influence over technology development and choice—and to go beyond the mere attempt to match skills to the latest technological fad. Strategies of skill reinterpretation must be amended to support the work of the future, promoting workers' skills as crucial to technological progress by reestablishing skill development as a protected worker right.

MEDICINE'S MACHINE LEARNING PROBLEM
Rachel Thomas

DATA SCIENCE IS REMAKING countless aspects of society, and medicine is no exception. The range of potential applications is already large and only growing by the day. Machine learning is now being used to determine which patients are at high risk of disease and need greater support (sometimes with racial bias), to discover which molecules may lead to promising new drugs, to search for cancer in X-rays (sometimes with gender bias), and to classify tissue on pathology slides. Last year MIT researchers trained an algorithm that was more accurate at predicting the presence of cancer within five years of a mammogram than techniques typically used in clinics, and a 2018 survey found that 84 percent of radiology clinics in the United States are using or plan to use machine learning software. The sense of excitement has been captured in popular books such as Eric Topol's *Deep Medicine: How Artificial Intelligence Can Make Healthcare Human Again* (2019). But despite the promise of these data-based innovations, proponents often overlook the special risks of datafying medicine in the age of artificial intelligence.

Consider one striking example that has unfolded during the pandemic. Numerous studies from around the world have found that significant numbers of COVID-19 patients—known as "long haulers"—experience symptoms that last for months. Good estimates range from 20 to 40 percent of all patients, depending on the study design, perhaps even higher. Yet a recent study from King's College London—picked up by CNN and the *Wall Street Journal*—gives a much lower estimate, claiming that only 2 percent of patients have symptoms for more than 12 weeks and only 4 percent have symptoms longer than 8 weeks. What explains the serious discrepancy? It turns out that the King's College study relies on data from a symptom tracking app that many long haulers quit using because it didn't take their symptoms or needs into account, resulting in a time-consuming and frustrating user experience. Long haulers are already dealing with disbelief from doctors, and the inaccurate results of this study may cause further harm—casting doubt on the reality of their condition.

This case is not an isolated exception, and it is not just an object lesson in bad data collection. It reflects a much deeper and more fundamental issue that all applications of data science and machine learning must reckon with: the way these technologies exacerbate imbalances of power. Data is not inert; it causes a doctor to mistakenly tell a patient that her dementia-like symptoms must just be due to a vitamin deficiency or stress. A software bug is not just an error in a line of code; it is a woman with cerebral palsy losing the home health aide she relies on in daily life. As others have argued, the ethics of AI turn crucially on whose voices are listened to and whose are sidelined. These problems are not easily fixed, for the same reason they exist in the first place: the people most impacted—those whose lives are changed by the outcome of an algorithm—have no power, just as they are so often ignored when the tech is being built. Anyone excited about the promise of machine learning for medicine must wrestle seriously with the perils.

As a starting point, we can take five principles to heart. First, it is crucial to acknowledge that medical data—like all data—can be incomplete, incorrect, missing, and biased. Second, we must recognize how machine learning systems can contribute to the centralization of power at the expense of patients and health care providers alike. Third, machine learning designers and adopters must not take new systems onboard without considering how they will interface with a medical system that is already disempowering and often traumatic for patients. Fourth, machine learning must not dispense with domain expertise—and we must recognize that patients have their own expertise distinct from that of doctors. Finally, we need to move the conversation around bias and fairness to focus on power and participation.

Flaws in Medical Data

BIAS IS ENDEMIC in medicine. One recent example concerns pulse oximeters, a crucial tool in clinical practice and an essential tool in the pandemic. Prompted by an essay in these pages, which detailed the way most oximeters are calibrated on patients with light skin, a recent study in the *New England Journal of Medicine* found that Black patients are three times as likely as white patients to get misleading readings, which may impact clinical outcomes. Fitbit heart rate monitors, currently used in over 300 clinical trials, are also less accurate on people of color. Scores of studies show that women and people of color receive less pain medication, lower quality of care, and longer time delays to treatment. Women's pain is often misattributed by doctors as psychological, resulting in women who report pain being prescribed antidepressants (when they haven't reported symptoms of depression) rather than painkillers. And similar findings have been observed for race: "A 2012 meta-analysis of twenty years of published research found that Black patients were 22 percent less likely than whites to get any pain medication and 29 percent less likely to be treated with opioids," a BBC article puts it.

These biases—among many others—can result in deeply flawed medical data. The observations, diagnoses, and decisions made by doctors are often treated as objective, but they are fallible, and flawed judgments result in flawed data. In most cases we do not have data directly recording what patients experience; instead those reports are filtered through a doctor's perception of their state. Any machine learning model relying on this data is at risk of replicating these biases, delays, and errors.

To take another important example of the way medical datasets may systematically misrepresent reality, diagnosis delays are common for many illnesses, leading to incomplete and incorrect data at any one snapshot in time. On average it takes five years and five doctors for patients with autoimmune diseases such as multiple sclerosis and lupus to get a diagnosis; three-quarters of these patients are women, and half report being labeled as chronic complainers in the early stages of disease. Diagnosis of Crohn's disease takes twelve months for men and twenty months for women, while diagnosis for Ehlers-Danlos syndrome takes four years for men and sixteen years for women. Consider how many patients have not received an accurate diagnosis yet or who give up before ever finding one. This leads to incomplete and missing data.

There is also a pernicious cycle around missing medical data for poorly understood diseases: doctors disbelieve patients about their symptoms and dismiss them as anxious or complaining too much. This leads to undercounting how many people are impacted by certain symptoms or diseases, which in turn makes it harder to make a case for increased funding; the diseases may remain poorly understood and patients continue to be disbelieved.

These are just some of the ways the quality of medical data can be misleading or biased. In working with medical data, it is imperative to consider tests that aren't ordered and notes that aren't recorded. And it is essential to listen to patients about the ways their data is incomplete, incorrect, or missing. Despite the rise of so-called "debiasing" algorithms, all datasets are biased, and the only way we can understand how is through qualitative work: inspecting how the dataset was gathered, listening to those who have firsthand experience and will be most impacted, and examining the relevant history and social structures.

The Centralization of Power

TOO OFTEN machine learning has the effect of further concentrating and centralizing power away from those most affected by the technology. The risk arises because machine learning can be used cheaply at massive scale; it can amplify biases across entire systems where they would otherwise be more localized; it can be used to evade responsibility; it can be implemented with no system for recourse and no way to identify mistakes; and it can create pernicious feedback loops. We have seen this across a range of domains already: governments using facial recognition to identify protesters; corporations using surveillance to track and even fire employees; the "great decoupling" of income and productivity (in which record corporate profits go to an ever smaller slice of executives); U.S. Immigration and Customs Enforcement misappropriating datasets; and job seekers subjected to degrading, time-consuming algorithms. These impacts are not experienced uniformly by all. We need to consider carefully how this dynamic could play out as machine learning is implemented within medicine.

In 2018 the *Verge* investigated an algorithm used in over half of U.S. states to determine how much health care people receive. When it was implemented in Arkansas, there was an error in the code that incorrectly and drastically cut health care for people with cerebral palsy. No explanations were given, and there was no easy way to appeal the cuts. For instance, Tammy Dobbs, a woman with cerebral palsy who needs an aide to help her carry out daily tasks such as getting out of bed, had her hours of help suddenly reduced by twenty-four hours a week. Eventually, a court case revealed that there were mistakes in the software implementation of the algorithm, negatively impacting people with diabetes or cerebral palsy. Dobbs and many others who rely on these health care benefits live in fear that they could again be cut suddenly and inexplicably.

We are still in the early days of widespread implementation of machine learning in medicine, and it is likely only a matter of time until we see examples of centralization of power and potential harms due to opaque algorithms and the lack of recourse that often accompanies machine learning implementations—particularly when they are used as cost-cutting measures, wrongly assumed to be error-free, and implemented without clear mechanisms for validation, correction, and ongoing oversight.

How Machine Learning Fits into an Already Distressing System

WE CAN'T UNDERSTAND how data and machine learning will impact medicine without first understanding how patients experience the medical system now. Professionally, I study how machine learning can amplify harms in other complex systems with big power differences. I have also studied the research on medical bias in particular, read hundreds of patients accounts, and am familiar with the medical system firsthand. I once went to the ER after several days of the worst pain of my life. No tests were given; I was discharged and told to take aspirin. I remember sobbing at the gap between my excruciating pain and the doctor's assessment. A few days later I went to a different ER, where an MRI was ordered. As soon as the results came back I was transferred to the neuro-ICU immediately, and I had brain surgery the next week.

Since then, I have had a life-threatening brain infection and a second brain surgery, and I continue to live with the long-term effects. My initial ER visit is just one of many times that I have been dismissed by medical professionals. Scores of patient accounts and research studies confirm that my experience is not unique. In a powerful comic, Aubrey Hirsch shares her experience waiting six years to get an accurate diagnosis for Graves' disease; she developed permanent damage to her bones, eyes, and heart during that time. She experienced debilitating symptoms, yet numerous doctors dismissed her as just an "anxious" young woman.

Such accounts are not exceptional in the history of medicine but more like the rule, including everything from dismissing women's illnesses as hysteria to the Tuskegee syphilis trials, in which Black men were denied a well-proven treatment for decades. The threads of history wind through to the present. How many patients still don't have accurate diagnoses? How many are still being dismissed and disbelieved? And how many patients don't have the resources to go to that additional ER, to keep seeking out doctors after years of dismissal? All these forms of ignorance and bias are reflected in medical data. Machine learning systems must consider how they interface with an already flawed and distressing medical system.

What Counts as Medical Expertise

DOMAIN EXPERTISE IS CRUCIAL for any applied machine learning project. Radiologists working in deep learning, for example, have discovered dataset issues with incorrectly labeled chest X-rays that those without a medical background would not have recognized on their own. However, it is often assumed that for medicine, the knowledge and experience of doctors is the only domain expertise there is. This is false. While the knowledge of doctors is of course essential, patients have a set of skills and expertise that is distinct but just as essential. Patients know what they are experiencing: what it is like to feel pain, what it is like to navigate a demoralizing health care system. As a patient it is not your pain or symptoms that matter on their own but the extent to which you can make them legible to providers and the tools they use. Patients must often strategize to try to avoid having their symptoms dismissed: to appear sick, but not in a way that a doctor may think they are faking it. Race, gender, class, weight, sexuality, and many other factors impact how patients are perceived and what contortions may be required to try to be taken seriously.

Many patients, particularly with rare or not widely understood illnesses, actively read medical papers, and in some cases will be more familiar with recent, relevant medical literature than some doctors. COVID-19 long-haulers, for example, many of whom have experience as data scientists and researchers, self-organized their own research study in April that made discoveries that mainstream medical research did not uncover until six months later. Doctors may inadvertently give inaccurate information due to being less familiar with recent developments outside their specialization and because unreasonable time constraints often make it impossible to adequately synthesize details of a medical history. Medical machine learning runs the risk of encoding assumptions and current ways of knowing into systems that will be significantly harder to change later. We are at a crucial inflection point with the machine learning revolution, where decisions made now will reverberate for decades to come.

From Bias and Fairness to Power and Participation

EVEN WHEN PROBLEMS with machine learning are brought to light, developers often propose "solutions" that involve mere tweaks to code, with no reckoning with the power dynamics at play and no inclusion of the people most impacted.

Fortunately, these concepts of power and participation are gaining more attention, through efforts by researchers, reporters, and activists such as Khari Johnson's reporting and the Participatory Approaches to Machine Learning (PAML) workshop, held this summer at the International Conference on Machine Learning, one of the premier academic machine learning conferences. As the PAML workshop organizers wrote:

> The fields of algorithmic fairness and human-centered [machine learning] often focus on centralized solutions, lending increasing power to system designers and operators, and less to users and affected populations. . . . We wish to consider a new set of technical formulations for the machine learning community on the subject of more democratic, cooperative, and participatory [machine learning] systems.

Researchers in this area have talked about the need to move beyond explainability (seeking explanations for how an algorithm made a decision) to recourse (giving those impacted concrete actions they could take to change the outcome) and to move beyond transparency (insight to how an algorithm works) to contestability (allowing people to challenge it). In a recent op-ed for *Nature*, AI researcher Pratyusha Kalluri urges that we replace the question, "Is this AI fair?" with the question, "How does this shift power?"

These issues are especially crucial in the domain of medicine, where so many patients are already disempowered, and the risk of further centralizing power could lead to great harm. While machine learning may indeed help to bring huge benefits to medicine, patients must be centered and their expertise must be closely listened to. As AI researcher Inioluwa Deborah Raji wrote in July: "Data are not bricks to be stacked, oil to be drilled, gold to be mined, opportunities to be harvested. Data

are humans to be seen, maybe loved, hopefully taken care of."
We must insist on mechanisms for ensuring power and participation
now in order to ensure the human side of health care is not further
eroded in medicine's machine learning revolution.

THE PAST AND FUTURE OF AI

Kenneth Taylor

Editors' Note: Philosopher Kenneth Taylor passed away on December 2, 2019. Boston Review *is proud to publish this essay in collaboration with his estate.*

Among the works of man, which human life is rightly employed in perfecting and beautifying, the first in importance surely is man himself. Supposing it were possible to get houses built, corn grown, battles fought, causes tried, and even churches erected and prayers said, by machinery—by automatons in human form—it would be a considerable loss to exchange for these automatons even the men and women who at present inhabit the more civilized parts of the world, and who assuredly are but starved specimens of what nature can and will produce. Human nature is not a machine to be built after a model, and set to do exactly the work prescribed for it, but a tree, which requires to grow and develop itself on all sides, according to the tendency of the inward forces which make it a living thing.

—John Stuart Mill, *On Liberty* (1859)

SOME BELIEVE that we are on the cusp of a new age. The day is coming when practically *anything* that a human can do—at least anything that the labor market is willing to *pay* a human being a decent wage to do—will soon be doable more efficiently and cost effectively by some AI-driven automated device. If and when that day does arrive, those who own the means of production will feel ever increasing pressure to discard human workers in favor of an artificially intelligent work force. They are likely to do so as unhesitatingly as they have always set aside outmoded technology in the past.

To be sure, technology has disrupted labor markets before. But until now, even the most far reaching of those disruptions have been relatively easy to adjust to and manage. That is because new technologies have heretofore tended to displace workers from old jobs that either no longer needed to be done—or at least no longer needed to be done by humans—into either entirely new jobs that were created by the new technology, or into old jobs for which the new technology, directly or indirectly, caused increased demand.

This time things may be radically different. Thanks primarily to AI's presumed potential to equal or surpass every human cognitive achievement or capacity, it may be that many humans will be driven out of the labor market altogether.

Yet it is not necessarily time to panic. Skepticism about the impact of AI is surely warranted on inductive grounds alone. Way back in 1956, at the Dartmouth Summer Research Project on Artificial Intelligence, an event that launched the first AI revolution, the assembled gaggle of AI pioneers—all ten of them—breathlessly anticipated that the mystery of fully general artificial intelligence

Taylor

could be solved within a couple of decades at most. In 1961 Hyman Minsky, for example, was confidently proclaiming, "We are on the threshold of an era that will be strongly influenced, and quite possibly dominated, by intelligent problem-solving machines." Well over a half century later, we are still waiting for the revolution to be fully achieved.

AI has come a long way since those early days: it is now a very big deal. It is a major focus of academic research, and not just among computer scientists. Linguists, psychologists, the legal establishment, the medical establishment, and a whole host of others have gotten into the act in a very big way. AI may soon be talking to us in flawless and idiomatic English, counseling us on fundamental life choices, deciding who gets imprisoned for how long, and diagnosing our most debilitating diseases. AI is also big business. The worldwide investment in AI technology, which stood at something like $12 billion in 2018, will top $200 billion by 2025. Governments are hopping on the AI bandwagon. The Chinese envision the development of a trillion-dollar domestic AI industry in the relatively near term. They clearly believe that the nation that dominates AI will dominate the world. And yet, a sober look at the current state of AI suggests that its promise and potential may still be a tad oversold.

Excessive hype is not confined to the distant past. One reason for my own skepticism is the fact that in recent years the AI landscape has come to be progressively more dominated by AI of the newfangled "deep learning" variety, rather than by AI of the more or less passé "logic-based symbolic processing" variety—affectionately known in some quarters, and derisively known in others, as GOFAI (Good Old Fashion Artificial Intelligence).

It was mostly logic-based, symbolic processing GOFAI that so fired the imaginations of the founders of AI back in 1956. Admittedly, to the extent that you measure success by where time, money, and intellectual energy are currently being invested, GOFAI looks to be something of a dead letter. I don't want to rehash the once hot theoretical and philosophical debates over which approach to AI—logic-based symbolic processing, or neural nets and deep learning—is the more intellectually satisfying approach. Especially back in the '80s and '90s, those debates raged with what passes in the academic domain as white-hot intensity. They no longer do, but not because they were decisively settled in favor of deep learning and neural nets more generally. It's more that machine learning approaches, mostly in the form of deep learning, have recently achieved many impressive results. Of course these successes may not be due entirely to the anti-GOFAI character of these approaches. Even GOFAI has gotten into the machine learning act with, for example, Bayesian networks. The more relevant divide may be between probabilistic approaches of various sorts and logic-based approaches.

However exactly you divide up the AI landscape, it is important to distinguish what I call AI-as-engineering from what I call AI-as–cognitive science. AI-as-engineering isn't particularly concerned with mimicking the precise way in which the human mind-brain does distinctively human things. The strategy of engineering machines that do things that are in some sense intelligent, even if they do what they do in their own way, is a perfectly fine way to pursue artificial intelligence. AI-as–cognitive science, on the other hand, takes as its primary goal that of understanding and perhaps reverse engineering the human mind. AI pretty much began its life by being in this business, perhaps because human intelligence was the only robust model of intelligence it had to work with. But these days, AI-as-engineering is where the real money turns out to be.

Though there is certainly value in AI-as-engineering, I confess to still have a hankering for AI-as–cognitive science. And that explains why I myself still feel the pull of the old logic-based symbolic processing approach. Whatever its failings, GOFAI had as one among its primary goals that of reverse engineering the human mind. Many decades later, though we have definitely made some progress, we still haven't gotten all that far with that particular endeavor. When it comes to that daunting task, just about all the newfangled probability and statistics-based approaches to AI—most especially deep learning, but even approaches that have more in common with GOFAI like Bayesian nets—strike me as if not exactly nonstarters, then at best only a very small part of the truth. Probably the complete answer will involve some synthesis of older approaches and newer approaches and perhaps even approaches we haven't even thought of yet. Unfortunately, however, although there are a few voices starting to sing such an ecumenical tune, neither ecumenicalism nor intellectual modesty are exactly the rage these days.

BACK WHEN the competition over competing AI paradigms was still a matter of intense theoretical and philosophical dispute, one of the advantages often claimed on behalf of artificial neural nets over logic-based symbolic approaches was that the former but not the latter were directly neuronally inspired. By directly modeling its computational atoms and computational networks on neurons and their interconnections, the thought went, artificial neural nets were bound to be truer to how the actual human brain does its computing than its logic-based symbolic processing competitor could ever hope to be.

This is not the occasion to debate such claims at length. My own hunch is that there is little reason to believe that deep learning actually holds the key to finally unlocking the mystery of general purpose, humanlike intelligence. Despite being neuronally inspired, many of the most notable successes of the deep learning paradigm depend crucially on the ability of deep learning architectures to do something that the human brain isn't all that good at: extracting highly predictive, though not necessarily deeply explanatory, patterns on the basis of being trained up, via either supervised or unsupervised learning, on huge data sets, consisting, from the machine-eye point of view, of a plethora of weakly correlated feature bundles, without the aid of any top-down direction or built-in worldly knowledge. That is an extraordinarily valuable and computationally powerful technique for AI-as-engineering. And it is perfectly suited to the age of massive data, since the successes of deep learning wouldn't be possible without big data.

It's not that we humans are pikers at pattern extraction. As a species we do remarkably well at it, in fact. But I doubt that the capacity for statistical analysis of huge data sets is the core competence on which all other aspects of human cognition are ultimately built. But here's the thing. Once you've invented a really cool new hammer—which deep learning very much is—it's a very natural human tendency to start looking for nails to hammer everywhere. Once you are on the lookout for nails everywhere, you can expect to find a lot more of them than you might have at first thought, and you are apt to find some of them in some pretty surprising places.

But if it's really AI-as–cognitive science that you are interested in, it's important not to lose sight of the fact that it may take a bit more than our cool new deep learning hammer to build a humanlike mind. You can't let your obsession with your cool new hammer make you lose sight of the fact that in some domains, the human mind seems to deploy quite a different trick from the main sorts of tricks that are at the core not only of deep learning but also other statistical paradigms (some of which, again, are card carrying members of the GOFAI family). In particular the human mind is often able to learn quite a lot from relatively little and comparatively impoverished data. This remarkable fact has led some to conjecture that human mind must come antecedently equipped with a great deal of endogenous, special-purpose, task specific cognitive structure and content. If true, that alone would suffice to make the human mind rather unlike your typical deep learning architecture.

Indeed, deep learning takes quite the opposite approach. A deep learning network may be trained up to represent words, say, as points in a micro-featural vector space of, say, three hundred dimensions, and on the basis of such representations, it might learn, after many epochs of training, on a really huge data set, to make the sort of pragmatic inferences—from say, "John ate some of the cake" to "John did not eat all of the cake"—that humans make quickly, easily, and naturally, without a lot of focused training of the sort required by deep learning and similar such approaches. The point is that deep learning can learn to do various cool things—things that one might once have thought only human beings can do—and although they can do some of those things quite well, it still seems highly unlikely that they do those cool things in precisely the way that we humans do.

I STRESS AGAIN, though, that if you are not primarily interested in AI-as–cognitive science, but solely in AI-as-engineering, you are free to care not one whit whether deep learning architectures and their cousins hold the ultimate key to understanding human cognition in all its manifestations. You are free to embrace and exploit the fact that such architectures are not just good, but extraordinarily good, at what they do, at least when they are given large enough data sets to work with. Still, in thinking about the future of AI, especially in light of both our darkest dystopian nightmares and our brightest utopian dreams, it really does matter whether we are envisioning a future shaped by AI-as-engineering or AI-as–cognitive science. If I am right that there are many mysteries about the human mind that currently dominant approaches to AI are ill equipped to help us solve, then to the extent that such approaches continue to dominate AI into the future, we are very unlikely to be inundated anytime soon with a race of thinking robots—at least not if we mean by "thinking" that

Taylor

peculiar thing that we humans do, done in precisely the way that we humans do it.

Deep learning and its cousins may do what they do better than we could possibly do what they do. But that doesn't imply that they do what we do better than we do what we do. If so, then, at the very least, we needn't fear, at least not yet, that AI will radically outpace humans in our most characteristically human modes of cognition. Nor should we expect the imminent arrival of the so-called singularity in which human intelligence and machine intelligence somehow merge to create a super intelligence that surpasses the limits of each. Given that we still haven't managed to understand the full bag of tricks our amazing minds deploy, we haven't the slightest clue as to what such a merger would even plausibly consist in.

Nonetheless it would still be a major mistake to lapse into a false sense of security about the potential impact of AI on the human world. Even if current AI is far from being the holy grail of a science of mind that finally allows us to reverse engineer it, it will still allow us to engineer extraordinarily powerful cognitive networks, as I will call them, in which human intelligence and artificial intelligence of some kind or other play quite distinctive roles. Even if we never achieve a single further breakthrough in AI-as–cognitive science, from this day forward, for as long as our species endures, the task of managing what I will call the division of cognitive labor between human and artificial intelligence within engineered cognitive networks will be with us to stay. And it will almost certainly be a rather fraught and urgent matter. And this will be thanks in large measure to the power of AI-as-engineering rather than to the power of AI-as–cognitive science.

Indeed, there is a distinct possibility that AI-as-engineering may eventually reduce the role of human cognitive labor within future cognitive networks to the bare minimum. It is that possibility—not the possibility of the so-called singularity or the possibility that we will soon be surrounded by a race of free, autonomous, creative, or conscious robots, chafing at our undeserved dominance over them— that should now and for the foreseeable future worry us most. Long before the singularity looms even on some distant horizon, the sort of AI technology that AI-as-engineering is likely to give us already has the potential to wreak considerable havoc on the human world. It will not necessarily do so by superseding human intelligence, but simply by displacing a great deal of it within various engineered cognitive networks. And if that's right, it simply won't take the arrival of anything close to full-scale super AI, as we might call it, to radically disrupt, for good or for ill, the built cognitive world.

Start with the fact that much of the cognitive work that humans are currently tasked to do within extant cognitive networks doesn't come close to requiring the full range of human cognitive capacities to begin with. A human mind is an awesome cognitive instrument, one of the most powerful instruments that nature has seen fit to evolve. (At least on our own lovely little planet! Who knows what sorts of minds evolution has managed to design on the millions upon millions of mind-infested planets that must be out there somewhere?) But stop and ask yourself, how much of the cognitive power of her amazing human mind does a coffee house barista, say, really use in her daily work?

Taylor

Not much, I would wager. And precisely for that reason, it's not hard to imagine coffee houses of the future in which more and more of the cognitive labor that needs doing within them is done by AI finely tuned to cognitive loads they will need to carry within such cognitive networks. More generally, it is abundantly clear that much of the cognitive labor that needs doing within our total cognitive economy that now happens to be performed by humans is cognitive labor for which we humans are often vastly overqualified. It would be hard to lament the off-loading of such cognitive labor onto AI technology.

But there is also a flip side. The twenty-first-century economy is already a highly data-driven economy. It is likely to become a great deal more so, thanks—among other things—to the emergence of the Internet of things. The built environment will soon be even more replete with so-called "smart" devices. And these smart devices will constantly be collecting, analyzing, and sharing reams and reams of data on every human being who interacts with them. It will not be just the usual suspects, like our computers, smart phones, or smart watches, that are so engaged. It will be our cars, our refrigerators, indeed every system or appliance in every building in the world. There will be data-collecting monitors of every sort—heart monitors, sleep monitors, baby monitors. There will be smart roads, smart train tracks. There will be smart bridges that constantly monitor their own state and automatically alert the transportation department when they need repair. Perhaps they will shut themselves down and spontaneously reroute traffic while they are waiting for the repair crews to arrive. It will require an extraordinary amount of cognitive labor to keep such a built environment running smoothly. And for much of that cognitive labor, we humans are vastly underqualified. Try, for example, running a data mining operation using nothing but human brain power. You'll see pretty quickly that human brains are not at all the right tool for the job, I would wager.

PERHAPS WHAT SHOULD REALLY WORRY US, I am suggesting, is the possibility that the combination of our overqualification for certain cognitive labor and underqualification for other cognitive labor will leave us open to something of an AI pincer attack. AI-as-engineering may give us the power to design cognitive networks in which each node is exquisitely fine-tuned to the cognitive load it is tasked to carry. Since distinctively human intelligence will often be either too much or too little for the task at hand, future cognitive networks may assign very little cognitive labor to humans. And that is precisely how it might come about that the demand for human cognitive labor within the overall economy may be substantially diminished. How should we think about the advance of AI in light of its capacity to allow us to reimagine and reengineer our cognitive networks in this way? That is the question I address in the remainder of this essay.

There may be lessons to be learned from the ways that we have coped with disruptive technological innovations of the past. So perhaps we should begin by looking backward rather than forward. The first thing to say is that many innovations of the past are now widely seen as good things, at least on balance. They often spared humans work that paid dead-end wages, or work that was dirty and dangerous, or work that was the source of mind-numbing drudgery.

But we should be careful not to overstate the case for the liberating power of new technology, lest that lure us to into a misguided complacency about what is to come. Even looking backward, we can see that new and disruptive technologies have sometimes been the culprits in increasing rather than decreasing the drudgery and oppressiveness of work. They have also served to rob work of a sense of meaning and purpose. The assembly line is perhaps the prime example. The rise of the assembly line doubtlessly played a vital role in making the mass production and distribution of all manner of goods possible. It made the factory worker vastly more productive than, say, the craftsman of old. In so doing, it increased the market for mass-produced goods, while simultaneously diminishing the market for the craftsman's handcrafted goods. As such, it played a major role in increasing living standards for many. But it also had the effect of turning many human agents into mere appendages within a vast, impersonal, and relentless mechanism of production.

All things considered, it would be hard to deny that trading in skilled craftsmanship for unskilled or semiskilled factory labor was a good thing. I do not intend to relitigate that choice here. But it is worth asking whether all things really were considered—and considered not just by those who owned the means of production but collectively by all the relevant stakeholders. I am no historian of political economy, but I venture the conjecture that the answer to that question is a resounding no. More likely than not, disruptive technological change was simply foisted on society as a whole, primarily by those who owned and controlled the means of production, and primarily to serve their own profit, with little, if any, intentionality or democratic deliberation and participation on the part of a broader range of stakeholders.

Given the disruptive potential even of AI-as-engineering, we cannot afford to leave decisions about the future development and deployment of even this sort of AI solely in the hands of those who stand to make vast profits from its use. This time around, we have to find a way to ensure that all relevant stakeholders are involved and that we are more intentional and deliberative in our decision-making than we were about the disruptive technologies of the past.

I am not necessarily advocating the sort of socialism that would require the means of production to be collectively owned or regulated. But even if we aren't willing to go so far as collectively seizing the machines, as it were, we must get past the point of treating not just AI but all technology as a thing unto itself, with a life of its own, whose development and deployment is entirely independent of our collective will. Technology is never self-developing or self-deploying. Technology is always and only developed and deployed by humans, in various political, social, and economic contexts. Ultimately, it is and must be entirely up to us, and up to us collectively, whether, how, and to what end it is developed and deployed. As soon as we lose sight of the fact that it is up to us collectively to determine whether AI is to be developed and deployed in a way that enhances the human world rather than diminishes it, it is all too easy to give in to either utopian cheerleading or dystopian fear-mongering. We need to discipline ourselves not to give in to either prematurely. Only such discipline will afford us the space to consider various tradeoffs deliberatively, reflectively, and intentionally.

Utopian cheerleaders for AI often blithely insist that it is more likely to decrease than increase the amount of dirt, danger, or drudgery to which human workers are subject. As long as AI is not turned against us—and why should we think that it would be?—it will not eliminate the work for which we humans are best suited, but only the work that would be better left to machines in the first place.

I do not mean to dismiss this as an entirely unreasonable thought. Think of coal mining. Time was when coal mining was extraordinarily dangerous and dirty work. Over 100,000 coal miners died in mining accidents in the United States alone during the twentieth century—not to mention the amount of black lung disease they suffered. Thanks largely to automation and computer technology, including robotics and AI technology, your average twenty-first-century coal industry worker relies a lot more on his or her brains than on mere brawn and is subject to a lot less danger and dirt than earlier generations of coal miners were. Moreover, it takes a lot fewer coal miners to extract more coal than the coal miners of old could possibly hope to extract.

To be sure, thanks to certain other forces having nothing to do with the AI revolution, the number of people dedicated to extracting coal will likely diminish even further in the relatively near term. But that just goes to show that even if we could manage to tame AI's effect on the future of human work, we've still got plenty of other disruptive challenges to face as we begin to reimagine and reengineer the made human world. But that just gives us even more reason to be intentional, reflective, and deliberative in thinking about the development and deployment of new technologies. Whatever one technology can do on its own to disrupt the human world, the interactive effects of multiple apparently independent technologies can greatly amplify the total level of disruption to which we may be subject.

I suppose that, if we had to choose, utopian cheerleading would at least feel more satisfying and uplifting than dystopian fear-mongering. But we shouldn't be blind to the fact that any utopian buzz we may fall into while contemplating the future may serve to blind us to the fact that AI is very likely to transform—perhaps radically—our collective intuitive sense of where the boundary between work better consigned to machines and work best left to us humans should fall in the first place. The point is that that boundary is likely to be drawn, erased, and redrawn by the progress of AI. And as our conception of the proper boundary evolves, our conception of what we humans are here for is likely to evolve right along with it.

The upshot is clear. If it is only relative to our sense of where the boundary is properly drawn that we could possibly know whether to embrace or recoil from the future, then we are now currently in no position to judge on behalf of our future selves which outcomes are to be embraced and which are to be feared. Nor, perhaps, are we entitled to insist that our current sense of where the boundary should be drawn should remain fixed for all time and circumstances.

Taylor

TO DRIVE THIS LAST POINT HOME, it will help to consider three different cognitive networks in which AI already plays, or soon can be expected to play, a significant role: the air traffic control system, the medical diagnostic and treatment system, and what I'll call the ground traffic control system. My goal in so doing is to examine some subtle ways in which our sense of proper boundaries may shift.

Begin with the air traffic control system, one of the more developed systems in which brain power and computer power have been jointly engineered to cooperate in systematically discharging a variety of complex cognitive burdens. The system has steadily evolved over many decades into a system in which a surprising amount of cognitive work is done by software rather than humans. To be sure, there are still many humans involved. Human pilots sit in every cockpit and human brains monitor every air traffic control panel. But it is fair to say that humans, especially human pilots, no longer really fly airplanes on their own within this vast cognitive network. It's really the system as a whole that does the flying. Indeed, it's only on certain occasions, and on an as-needed basis, that the human beings within the system are called upon to do anything at all. Otherwise, they are mostly along for the ride.

This particular human–computer cognitive network works extremely well for the most part. It is extraordinarily safe in comparison with travel by automobile. And it is getting safer all the time. Its ever-increasing safety would seem to be in large measure due to the fact that more and more of the cognitive labor done within the system is being offloaded onto machine intelligence and taken away from human intelligence. Indeed, I would hazard the guess that almost no increases in safety have resulted from taking burdens away from algorithms and machines and giving them to humans instead.

To be sure, this trend started long before AI had reached anything like its current level of sophistication. But with the coming of age of AI-as-engineering, you can expect that the trend will only accelerate. For example, starting in the 1970s, decades of effort went into building human-designed rules meant to provide guidance to pilots as to which maneuvers executed in which order would enable them to avoid any possible or pending midair collision. In more recent years, engineers have been using AI techniques to help design a new collision avoidance system that will make possible a significant increase in air safety. The secret to the new system is that instead of leaving the discovery of optimal rules of the airways to human ingenuity, the problem has been turned over to the machines. The new system uses computational techniques to derive an optimized decision logic that deals with various sources of uncertainty and balances competing system objectives better than anything that we humans would likely think up on our own. The new system, called Airborne Collision Avoidance System (ACAS) X, promises to pay considerable dividends by reducing both the risks of midair collision and the need for alerts that call for corrective maneuvers in the first place.

In all likelihood the system will not be foolproof—probably no system will ever be. But in comparison with automobile travel, air travel is already extraordinarily safe. It's not because the physics makes flying inherently safer than driving. Indeed, there was a time when flying was much riskier than it currently is. What makes air travel so much safer than driving is primarily the differences between the cognitive networks within which each operates. In the ground traffic control system, almost none of the cognitive labor has been off-loaded onto intelligent machines. Within the air traffic control system, a great deal of it has.

To be sure, every now and then, the flight system will call on a human pilot to execute a certain maneuver. When it does, the system typically isn't asking for anything like expert opinion from the human. Though it may sometimes need to do that, in the course of its routine operations, the system relies hardly at all on the ingenuity or intuition of human beings, including human pilots. When the system does need a human pilot to do something, it usually just needs the human to expertly execute a particular sequence of maneuvers. Mostly things go right. Mostly the humans do what they are asked to do, when they are asked to do it. But it should come as no surprise that when things do go wrong, it is quite often the humans and not the machines that are at fault. Humans too often fail to respond, or they respond with the wrong maneuver, or they execute the needed maneuver but in an untimely fashion.

I have focused on the air traffic control system because it is a relatively mature and stable cognitive network in which a robust balance between human and machine cognitive labor has been achieved over time. Given its robustness and stability and the degree of safety it provides, it's pretty hard to imagine anyone having any degree of nostalgia for the days when the task of navigating the airways fell more squarely on the shoulders of human beings and less on machines. On the other hand, it is not at all hard to imagine a future in which the cognitive role of humans is reduced even further, if not entirely eliminated. No one would now dream of traveling on an airplane that wasn't furnished with the latest radar system or the latest collision avoidance software. Perhaps the day will soon come when no one would dream of traveling on an airplane piloted by, of all things, a human being rather than by a robotic AI pilot.

I suspect that what is true of the air traffic control system may eventually be true of many of the cognitive networks in which human and machine intelligence systematically interact. We may find that the cognitive labor that was once assigned to the human nodes has been given over to intelligent machines for narrow economic reasons alone—especially if we fail to engage in collective decision-making that is intentional, deliberative, and reflective and thereby leave ourselves to the mercy of the short-term economic interests of those who currently own and control the means of production.

We may comfort ourselves that even in such an eventuality, that which is left to us humans will be cognitive work of very high value, finely suited to the distinctive capacities of human beings. But I do not know what would now assure us of the inevitability of such an outcome. Indeed, it may turn out that there isn't really all that much that needs doing within such networks that is best done by human brains at all. It may be, for example, that within most engineered cognitive networks, the human brains that still have a place within them will mostly be along for the ride. Both possibilities are, I think, genuinely live options. And if I had to place a bet, I would bet that, for the foreseeable future, the total landscape of engineered cognitive networks will increasingly contain engineered networks of both kinds.

In fact, the two system I mentioned earlier—the medical diagnostic and treatment system and the ground transportation system—already provide evidence of my conjecture. Start with the medical diagnostic and treatment system. Note that a great deal of medical diagnosis involves expertise at interpreting the results of various forms of medical imaging. As things currently stand, it is mostly human beings who do the interpreting. But an impressive variety of machine learning algorithms that can do at least as well as humans are being developed at a rapid pace. For example, CheXNet, developed at Stanford, promises to equal or exceed the performance of human radiologists in the diagnosis of a wide variety of different diseases from X-ray scans. Partly because of the success of CheXNEt and other machine learning algorithms, Geoffrey Hinton, the founding father of deep learning, has come to regard radiologists as an endangered species. On his view, medical schools ought to stop training radiologists beginning right now.

Even if Hinton is right, that doesn't mean that all the cognitive work done by the medical diagnostic and treatment system will soon be done by intelligent machines. Though human-centered radiology may soon come to seem quaint and outmoded, there is, I think, no plausible short- to medium-term future in which human doctors are completely written out of the medical treatment and diagnostic system. For one thing, though the machines beat humans at diagnosis, we still outperform the machines when it comes to the treatment—perhaps because humans are much better at things like empathy than any AI system is now or is likely to be anytime soon. Still, even if the human doctors are never fully eliminated from the diagnostic and treatment cognitive network, it is likely that their enduring roles within such networks will evolve so much that human doctors of tomorrow will bear little resemblance to human doctors of today.

By contrast, there is a quite plausible near- to medium-term future in which human beings within the ground traffic control system are gradually reduced to the status of passengers. Someday in the not terribly distant future, our automobiles, buses, trucks, and trains will likely be part of a highly interconnected ground transportation system in which much of the cognitive labor is done by intelligent machines rather than human brains. The system will involve smart vehicles in many different configurations, each loaded with advanced sensors that allow them to collect, analyze, and act on huge stores of data, in coordination with each other, the smart roadways on which they travel, and perhaps some centralized information hub that is constantly monitoring the whole. Within this system, our vehicles will navigate the roadways and railways safely and smoothly with very little guidance from humans. Humans will be able to direct the system to get this or that cargo or passenger from here to there. But the details will be left to the system to work out without much, if any, human intervention.

Such a development, if and when it comes to fruition, will no doubt be accompanied by quantum leaps in safety and efficiency. But no doubt it would be a major source of a possibly permanent and steep decrease in the net demand for human labor of the sort that we referred to at the outset. All around the world, many millions of human beings make their living by driving things from one place to another. Labor of this sort has traditionally been rather secure. It cannot possibly be outsourced to foreign competitors. That is, you cannot transport beer, for example, from Colorado to Ohio by hiring a low-wage driver operating a truck in Beijing. But it may soon be the case that we can outsource such work after all. Not to foreign laborers but to intelligent machines, right here in our midst!

I END WHERE I BEGAN. The robots are coming. Eventually, they may come for every one of us. Walls will not contain them. We cannot outrun them. Nor will running faster than the next human being suffice to save us from them. Not in the long run. They are relentless, never breaking pace, never stopping to savor their latest prey before moving on to the next.

If we cannot stop or reverse the robot invasion of the built human world, we must turn and face them. We must confront hard questions about what will and should become of both them and us as we welcome ever more of them into our midst. Should we seek to regulate their development and deployment? Should we accept the inevitability that we will lose much work to them? If so, perhaps we should rethink the very basis of our economy. Nor is it merely questions of money that we must face. There are also questions of meaning. What exactly will we do with ourselves if there is no longer any economic demand for human cognitive labor? How shall we find meaning and purpose in a world without work?

These are the sort of questions that the robot invasion will force us to confront. It should be striking that these are also the questions presaged in my prescient epigraph from Mill. Over a century before the rise of AI, Mill realized that the most urgent question raised by the rise of automation would not be the question of whether automata could perform certain tasks faster or cheaper or more reliably than human beings might. Instead, the most urgent question is what we humans would become in the process of substituting machine labor for human labor. Would such a substitution enhance us or diminish us? That has, in fact, always been the most urgent question raised by disruptive technologies, though we have seldom recognized it.

This time around, may we face the urgent question head on. And may we do so collectively, deliberatively, reflectively, and intentionally.

CODING CARE

Anna Romina Guevarra

AT THE HEIGHT of the COVID-19 pandemic, Awakening Health Ltd. (AHL), a joint venture between two robotics companies, SingularityNET (SNET) and Hanson Robotics, introduced Grace, the first medical robot to have a lifelike human appearance. Grace provides acute medical and elder care by engaging patients in therapeutic interactions, cognitive stimulation, and gathering and managing patient data. By the end of 2021, Hanson Robotics hopes to be able to mass-produce a robot named Grace—adapted from an ealier model, Sophia—for the global market.

Though Grace is the first to look so much like a person, she is hardly the first medical robot: like Tommy, Yumi, Stevie, Ava, and Moxi, she is part of a growing cohort of robot caregivers working in hospitals and elder care facilities around the world. They do everything from bedside care and monitoring to stocking medical supplies, welcoming guests, and even cohosting karaoke nights for isolated residents. Together, they have been heralded as a solution to our pandemic woes.

In the last couple of years, the sale of professional service robots has increased by 32 percent ($11.2 billion) worldwide; the sale of assistance robots for the elderly increased by 17 percent ($91 million) between 2018 and 2019 alone. The unique challenges of safely delivering care and services during the COVID-19 pandemic have only increased their appeal. This is evidenced by the increased global reliance on robotic systems to disinfect surfaces, enforce mask-wearing and social distancing protocol, monitor patients' vital signs, deliver supplies and groceries, conduct virtual tours, and even facilitate commencement ceremonies.

But what does this ramping up of interest and investment in robotics mean for human workers?

In the short term, there is no question that while robots may provide some support to human workers and help minimize their exposure to unsafe conditions, they cannot replace their human counterparts. At the current level of robotics, total replacement would require an impossible degree of predictability of work environments. As one of the pioneers in the field of social robotics, Lucy Suchman, noted, "Robots work best when the world has been arranged in the way that they need it to be arranged." Robots can function very well in factories and warehouses because assembly-line work provides a uniform environment; in homes and health care facilities, such uniformity is more difficult to achieve.

In the long run, though, robots may not always be so limited. Thus, it is critical that we consider not only whether robots *can* replace human workers—since someday the answer will surely be "yes"—but also whether they *should*. Indeed, the very *attempt* at automation represented by Grace and her cohort not only raises questions about the nature of work in general, but specifically about what it means to do *care* work. What does it mean to take care of another human being? And, in turn, what does it mean for an algorithm to care?

These questions of whether to employ phenomenally expensive robotic systems are especially poignant given that the field of care work relies heavily on the labor of poor women of color, often immigrants, who have long been told *both* that civilization depends upon their work *and* that it is of little monetary value. In this sense, any discussion of the transformative potential of care robots must be tempered by the reality that, as Ai-jen Poo and Palak Shah point out, the foreseeable "future of work" is not automation. The future of work continues to be an "essential," low-wage workforce that is disproportionately comprised of women of color who often lack a living wage, workplace safety, paid sick and family leave, and adequate health care. In fact, health care workers have been among the hardest hit by the pandemic. The most recent data from the Centers for Disease Control report that, to date, 450,000 health care personnel have been infected by COVID-19, and more than 1,500 have died, mainly people of color. Since there is significant underreporting and not all data are available, these figures are likely lower than the reality.

Against the expectations of many futurists, automation will not automatically generate a more just labor market. That will only happen if labor justice becomes a condition of automation's adoption. Otherwise, it will merely compound the problem, adding another layer to the inequities experienced by those most socially and economically vulnerable.

This is because algorithms tend to replicate biases that already exist in our world. In recent years this has been documented by critics of artificial intelligence, such as Joy Buolamwini, Safiya Umoja Noble, and Ruha Benjamin, who have noted how algorithmic biases are reflected in everything from facial recognition systems' failure to identify people of color to the technological redlining of search results related to Black subjects. Taken together these amount to being a *New Jim Code* of systemic racial bias encoded in new technologies. While our knowledge of the inner workings of these systems is often occluded because their algorithms are propriety, the output is clear: the work of Buolamwini, Noble, Benjamin, and others leaves little doubt that racialized regimes undergird computational systems and machine learning. That these new technologies do all this while being perceived as neutral—because machines are thought incapable of bias—only exacerbates the problem.

To return to the example of Grace—the newer version of the robot Sophia adjusted to serve the health care sector—her makers claim that these robots promise to provide not only safety but also "human warmth, human connection," and will serve as an "autonomous extension of human expertise." By choosing to have Grace look like a white woman, however, the designers broadcast a particular understanding of human expertise that is both racialized and gendered. A similar bias can be seen in the case of a telepresence robot called EngKey, designed to help teachers in Philippine call centers remotely offer English language instruction to elementary school children in South Korea. The EngKey robot wheels around the South Korean classroom with a *white* avatar face, even though it is a Filipina teacher who is delivering the lessons. Developers of EngKey remark that the rationale for the white avatar is twofold: one, to minimize the confusion of users in terms of who they are interacting with, the human or the robot; and two, to reinforce the perceived global "authority" for teaching English. However, in so doing, roboticists intervene in the geopolitics of labor, reinforcing a global fantasy of the ideal of what a qualified worker looks like while effacing the actual laborer, who does not fit this ideal. And the "robot teachers," as they call themselves, are forced by this arrangement to operate via a vocabulary of innovation that reinforces whiteness as powerful even as this script exploits their own "Third World" labor. Robot teachers I spoke with articulated a profound sense of dissociation that arose from embodying a blond, white robot face while performing a kind of affective labor that was simultaneously disembodied and embodied, immobile and mobile. Notably, this was done not to guarantee successful language instruction—which certainly did not depend on such a cleaving—but rather in the name of creating a seamless integration between human and machine as demanded by the roboticists.

The android Erica, created by Japanese roboticist Hiroshi Ishiguro, is another example of how, in the pursuit of humanness, roboticists can reproduce gendered norms. Ishiguro hopes that Erica, currently still an early prototype, will help lead the way toward a world in which machines and humans coexist, with robots enhancing the lives of humans by doing the most tedious and undesirable kinds of work, including caring for the sick and elderly. But by programming Erica to simulate a "warm, gentle, and caring" affect, Ishiguro's team has doubled down on the ways in which this kind of care work is gendered. Thus, Erica's design is premised on the perception that the labor of caring for the world rests primarily on the backs of women who will provide warmth and gentleness, while easing the burden and relieving the suffering of humanity. Erica is also designed to adhere to conventional standards of gendered beauty. As Ishiguro notes, he designed Erica to be the "most beautiful" android, drawing on the amalgamated images of (his perception of) "thirty beautiful women." Apparently it isn't enough to be a female caretaking robot; you have to be a "beautiful" one as well.

Concerns about race in robotics extend not only to how robots look but also how they will interact with others. How will robots such as Grace and Erica recognize and interpret a diversity of faces? Will the racist assumptions that are likely baked into Grace's algorithms define the type of therapeutic interventions that patients will receive? AI facial recognition systems are notoriously bad, for example, at interpreting the emotional responses of people with darker skin tones. Some can't perceive the faces of people with darker skin at all, let alone understand their expressions. It gets worse from there. Benjamin found that one of the most popular tools used by health insurers to assess health risks defined a theoretical Black patient as having less risk than a white patient with the same health markers because of racial bias in the tool's algorithms. In other words, what we are seeing is the emergence of yet another oppressive system that structures social relations by advancing a mediated understanding and delivery of care work. Borrowing from Buolamwini's idea of a "coded gaze" in algorithms, I refer to this racist imbalance in health care AI as *coded care*.

The idea of *coded care* gives us a vocabulary for thinking about the potential harm of automating care work. Increasingly, using robots to automate care work is pitched as necessary to assist an aging population, minimize occupational hazards, and address the high turnover and burnout rate among caregivers. One study suggests that by 2030, there will be a shortage of 151,000 paid direct care workers and 3.8 million unpaid family caregivers. But given these concerns about coded care, whether robotic automation is the best way to address this shortage is debatable. Even assuming that empathy, emotional labor, and creativity *can* be mechanized anytime in the near future—which many roboticists doubt—outsourcing these kinds of care may have grave consequences for those receiving that care if racist and gendered biases in the code are not addressed.

Moreover, we must take seriously the question with which we began—what this will mean for human workers—and the insistence that labor justice must be a precondition for the adoption of automation. Because these decisions will disproportionately impact women and communities of color, they are likely to take a back seat to moneyed interests and the well-being of affluent white people. But caring is a unique kind of labor, and when care workers are mistreated, we all lose out. Recall EngKey's robot teachers, whose sense of disconnectedness from their students translated into affective labor that is mechanized, racialized, and gendered in ways that harm both teachers and students. The work that EngKey performs teaches its Korean students as much about the enviable power of white femininity as it does about English. Likewise will Grace, whose creators promise a technology that will "engage patients naturally and emotionally," actually deliver comfort, empathy, and kindness to those isolated during the pandemic, or only a simulacra of how its creators imagine femininity?

More than ever, as the pandemic provides justification for expanding the use of care robots such as Grace, we should be mindful of how these interventions are coded. We need to push for more equitable and accountable artificial intelligence, working with collectives such as the Algorithmic Justice League (AJL) to achieve this goal. The work of AJL and others reminds us that "who codes matters, how we code matters, and that we can code a better future." If we are serious about pursuing robot labor, then labor justice must be a precondition for automation. Otherwise the robots will only provide another excuse to ignore the inequities faced by human workers by simply replacing them and automating their labor.

We need to continue to explore the ethics of developing care robots, informed by critiques about current models of automation by researchers such as Pramod P. Khargonekar and Meera Sampath and what they propose as "socially responsible automation." This model of automation suggests that there are ways that businesses can pursue automation while simultaneously investing in training and building the skills of human workers to adapt to this technology-driven workplace. Thus, the idea is not to simply replace human workers with a more efficient technology but to develop a workplace where robots and human workers can truly coexist.

But more importantly, I propose that the ethics of developing care robots must be based on a framework of labor justice that continues to develop remedies to the structural inequities that govern the lives and labor of essential workers. This can be done by supporting and adopting Senator Elizabeth Warren and Congressman Ro Khanna's proposal for an Essential Workers Bill of Rights. The provisions of this bill would ensure that care workers are not only receiving a living wage and health care security, but that they also have access to childcare and paid sick and medical leave.

I do not think that we can imagine a society without both human workers and robots. So, as roboticists work on developing care technologies, we need to attend to how the racialized and gendered perceptions get coded into the design. We cannot solely address how best to simulate humanity, but must also center principles of justice and equity in designs for coding care. Only then will it be possible to produce algorithms that truly care.

CONTRIBUTORS

Rediet Abebe is Assistant Professor of Computer Science at the University of California, Berkeley, Junior Fellow at the Harvard Society of Fellows, and cofounder of Mechanism Design for Social Good and Black in AI.

Daron Acemoglu is Institute Professor at MIT. He is coauthor, with James A. Robinson, of *The Narrow Corridor: States, Societies, and the Fate of Liberty* and *Why Nations Fail: The Origins of Power, Prosperity, and Poverty*.

Aaron Benanav is a researcher at Humboldt University of Berlin and author of *Automation and the Future of Work*.

Erik Brynjolfsson is Jerry Yang and Akiko Yamazaki Professor and Senior Fellow at the Stanford Institute for Human-Centered AI, Director of the Stanford Digital Economy Lab, and coauthor, with Andrew McAfee, of *The Second Machine Age: Work, Progress, and Prosperity in a Time of Brilliant Technologies*.

Kate Crawford is Research Professor at the USC Annenberg School for Communication and Journalism, Inaugural Chair of AI and Justice at the École Normale Supérieure in Paris, and author of *Atlas of AI: Power, Politics, and the Planetary Costs of Artificial Intelligence*.

Andrea Dehlendorf is Executive Director of United for Respect. She has twenty-five years of experience organizing with people working in low-wage retail and service sector jobs.

Ryan Gerety is Senior Advisor at United for Respect, where she focuses on the economic and political implications of new technology.

Anna Romina Guevarra is Founding Director and Associate Professor of Global Asian Studies at the University of Illinois Chicago and a Public Voices Fellow of the OpEd Project. She is author of *Marketing Dreams and Manufacturing Heroes: The Transnational Labor Brokering of Filipino Workers*.

William S. Isaac is Research Scientist at DeepMind, where he focuses on fairness and governance of AI systems.

Maximilian Kasy is Associate Professor of Economics at the University of Oxford. His research lies at the intersection of economics and machine learning and focuses on the social context of statistics and AI.

Molly Kinder is David M. Rubenstein Fellow at the Brookings Institution's Metropolitan Policy Program.

Nichola Lowe is Professor of City and Regional Planning at the University of North Carolina, Chapel Hill, and author of *Putting Skill to Work: How to Create Good Jobs in Uncertain Times*.

Shakir Mohamed is Research Scientist at DeepMind, Associate Fellow at the Leverhulme Centre for the Future of Intelligence at the University of Cambridge, and Honorary Professor of University College London.

Lama Nachman is an Intel Fellow and Director of the Anticipatory Computing Lab at Intel Labs.

Marie-Therese Png is a PhD Candidate at the Oxford Internet Institute and a former Technology Policy Advisor at the UN Secretary-General's High-level Panel on Digital Cooperation.

Rob Reich is Professor of Political Science at Stanford University, helps to lead its Center for Ethics in Society and Institute for Human-Centered AI, and is coauthor, with Jeremy M. Weinstein and Mehran Sahami, of *System Error: Where Big Tech Went Wrong and How We Can Reboot*.

Daniel Susskind is Fellow in Economics at Oxford University, a Visiting Professor at King's College London, and author of *A World Without Work: Technology, Automation, and How We Should Respond*.

Kenneth Taylor was the Henry Waldgrave Stuart Professor of Philosophy at Stanford University, cofounder of the podcast Philosophy Talk, and author of many books, including *Reference and the Rational Mind* and *Truth and Meaning*.

Rachel Thomas is Founding Director of the Center for Applied Data Ethics at the University of San Francisco and cofounder of fast.ai.

Annette Zimmermann is Lecturer in Philosophy at the University of York and Technology & Human Rights Fellow at the Carr Center for Human Rights Policy at the Harvard Kennedy School.